Cornerstones of Comprehension — grade 4

Table of Contents

About This Book 2

Sports
Wings on His Feet 3
The Barefoot Boy from Brazil 8
Little Miss Moffitt 12

Famous People
A Boy Called Curly 16
Furry Friends of Billy Moon 20
A Notebook in His Pocket,
　Liberty on His Mind 24

Animals
Are You Blue? 28
The Dog Who Blazed the
　Westward Trail 33
Strange, Spooky Spiders 38

Oddities
It's Raining, It's Pouring, It's
　Hopping? 42
Watch Out for That Plant! 47
Attack of the Killer Space
　Potatoes 51

Real-Life Mysteries
Life On Mars? 55
Nessie, Caddy, and Champ 59
Bigfoot Walks! 63

Adventure
Flying With Spirit 67
10...9...8...Danger! 71
Disaster by the Bay 75

Managing Editor: Deborah T. Kalwat
Editor at Large: Diane Badden
Staff Editors: Becky S. Andrews, Denine T. Carter, Cayce Guiliano, Scott Lyons, Diane F. McGraw
Contributing Writers: Bonnie Baumgras, Jan Brennan, Colleen Dabney, Therese Durhman, Carol Felts, Rusty Fischer, Kim Griswell, Terry Healy, Kathleen Kopp, Kimberly Minafo, Kathleen Scavone
Copy Editors: Sylvan Allen, Karen Brewer Grossman, Karen L. Huffman, Amy Kirtley-Hill, Kristy Parton, Debbie Shoffner
Cover Artists: Nick Greenwood, Clevell Harris
Art Coordinator: Greg D. Rieves
Artists: Pam Crane, Theresa Lewis Goode, Nick Greenwood, Clevell Harris, Ivy L. Koonce, Sheila Krill, Clint Moore, Greg D. Rieves, Rebecca Saunders, Barry Slate, Stuart Smith, Donna K. Teal
Typesetters: Lynette Dickerson, Mark Rainey

President, The Mailbox Book Company™: Joseph C. Bucci
Director of Book Planning and Development: Chris Poindexter
Book Development Managers: Cayce Guiliano, Elizabeth H. Lindsay, Thad McLaurin, Susan Walker
Curriculum Director: Karen P. Shelton
Traffic Manager: Lisa K. Pitts
Librarian: Dorothy C. McKinney
Editorial and Freelance Management: Karen A. Brudnak
Editorial Training: Irving P. Crump
Editorial Assistants: Terrie Head, Hope Rodgers, Jan E. Witcher

www.themailbox.com

©2003 by THE EDUCATION CENTER, INC.
All rights reserved.
ISBN #1-56234-501-X

Except as provided for herein, no part of this publication may be reproduced or transmitted in any form or by any means, electronic or mechanical, including photocopying, recording, or storing in any information storage and retrieval system or electronic online bulletin board, without prior written permission from The Education Center, Inc. Permission is given to the original purchaser to reproduce patterns and reproducibles for individual classroom use only and not for resale or distribution. Reproduction for an entire school or school system is prohibited. Please direct written inquiries to The Education Center, Inc., P.O. Box 9753, Greensboro, NC 27429-0753. The Education Center®, The Mailbox®, the mailbox/post/grass logo, and The Mailbox Book Company™ are trademarks of The Education Center, Inc., and may be the subject of one or more federal trademark registrations. All other brand or product names are trademarks or registered trademarks of their respective companies.

Manufactured in the United States
10 9 8 7 6 5 4 3 2 1

Cornerstones of Comprehension — grade 4

Research reveals that the single most valuable activity for developing students' comprehension is reading itself. At its core, comprehension is an active process in which readers think about text and gain meaning from it. In order for students to build competence in comprehension, their reading should be purposeful and reflective. *Cornerstones of Comprehension* is a resource that provides the instructional frame-work to help your students build essential comprehension skills and achieve success in reading!

Comprehension Basics

Comprehension begins with what a student knows about a topic. It builds as a child reads and actively makes connections between new information and prior knowledge. Understanding is increased as the student organizes what he has read in relationship to what he already knows. To successfully comprehend, students need to master a variety of critical skills, such as constructing word meanings from context, predicting, determining main ideas and locating details to support them, sequencing, drawing conclusions, summarizing, and sensing an author's purpose. *Cornerstones of Comprehension* provides multiple opportunities for reinforcing these essential skills, resulting in increased learning and competence in reading.

About This Book

Eighteen high-interest reading selections, each accompanied by five activities and two to three reproducible skill sheets, are featured in this book. (See the unit features detailed below.) Each unit is clearly organized and highlights one of the following topics: sports, famous people, animals, oddities, real-life mysteries, and adventure. *Cornerstones of Comprehension* will help you help your students strengthen comprehension and achieve reading success, while promoting reading for enjoyment and information.

• Reading Selection

The grade-specific nonfiction reading selections may be used as read-alouds, for partner reading, or for independent reading. Each original selection was carefully crafted to reflect the interests and abilities of your fourth graders. Content-area text is written in a narrative style and contains eight to 12 highlighted key vocabulary words. All selections are reproducible.

• Skill-Based Activities

Five skill-based activities for use before, during, and after reading accompany each selection. Grade-appropriate skills within activities are clearly identified and explained. Critical skills are featured throughout the units, providing multiple opportunities to reinforce learning and build reading competence.

• Skill Sheets

Each unit includes two or three reproducible skill sheets tied to the reading selection and selected activities. Use these skill sheets to provide further practice with skills, or for informal assessment of comprehension skills.

Wings on His Feet

If you know about the flying slam dunk, then you know about Michael Jordan. Jordan flew into basketball history in 1984. That's the year the Chicago Bulls chose him to join their team. The rest is history!

At six feet six inches, Jordan could jump higher than players half a foot taller. He could wiggle and waggle around in the air. He could toss off shots that left other players shaking their heads. How did he do it? Jordan once said he sometimes felt like he had little wings on his feet. His success on the **court** didn't come from magic wings, though. It came from practice.

Michael grew up in a middle-class family in Wilmington, North Carolina. His parents taught all of their children to work hard. They told them not to waste their **talent.** Maybe that's why Michael and his brother, Larry, played so hard on their grass basketball court. They both wanted to be the best. Day after day, Michael and Larry pounded it out on the backyard court.

Michael tried out a lot of sports before he **settled** on basketball. He tried football, track, and baseball. He thought he was too short and skinny to play basketball. Even though he was small, Michael became one of the best players on his ninth-grade basketball team. He was quick and driven by a **will** to win. One of his friends said, "If it was a game of Horse and you beat him, you would have to play another game until he won. You didn't go home until he had won."

Michael could hardly believe it when he didn't make the **varsity** basketball team his **sophomore** year. He was upset, but he didn't stop. Instead, he worked even harder. He became the star player on the junior varsity team. He scored up to 40 points in a game. Varsity players came to the games to check out his moves. The next year he made the varsity team.

By the time he started playing on the varsity team, Michael had grown four inches. He decided to focus on basketball. He never let up on himself. He pushed his teammates to work as hard as he did. He also became a good student. He hoped to go to college when he finished high school.

After high school, Michael went to the University of North Carolina at Chapel Hill. Even he was surprised when he was chosen to start as shooting **guard.** His first season was a great success. He even made the winning shot at the national championship game. He left college before his last year to play for the National Basketball Association (NBA). He was afraid he'd be a flop. However, his hard work and will to win launched him right to the top.

During the 13 years that Jordan played with the Chicago Bulls, he was named the NBA Most Valuable Player five times. He earned the NBA record for highest career scoring average. He demanded the best of himself and other team members. With Jordan in the lead, the Bulls won six national championships. In 1996, he was named one of the greatest North American athletes of the 20th century.

Will there ever be a player better than Jordan? Jordan once said that somewhere out there is another kid who won't be afraid, a kid who will work hard and build on the example of those who have gone before. Maybe that kid will grow little wings on his feet and fly off to **fame,** just like Michael Jordan!

Wings on His Feet

Activities

1 Multiple-Meaning Words

Before reading, grab a basketball and get students into a game of identifying multiple-meaning words. Begin by having students scan the selection for words having several meanings. List the words on the chalkboard. Next, have students stand in a circle. Bounce the ball to a student volunteer. Have him choose a word, use it in a sentence, and then bounce the ball to a classmate. Direct that student to use the same word, but with an alternate meaning, in a sentence. Then have her bounce the ball to a third classmate, who chooses a new word. Continue in this manner until each student has had a turn. (Multiple-meaning words in the selection include *rest, court, dunk, will, play, launched, guard, shot,* and *right*).

2 Character

Guide students to identify character traits that helped Michael Jordan achieve success on the court. After reading the selection have the class brainstorm a list of Michael Jordan's traits, such as *determination, focus,* and *talent.* Then provide each student with scissors and a 12" x 18" sheet of light-colored construction paper. Have each student trace her foot and hands on the paper as shown and cut out the resulting pattern. Then have her write three character traits from the list, one on each section of the winged foot. For each listed trait, have her write a detail from the selection that supports it. Suspend each student's winged foot over her desk using a length of string or yarn.

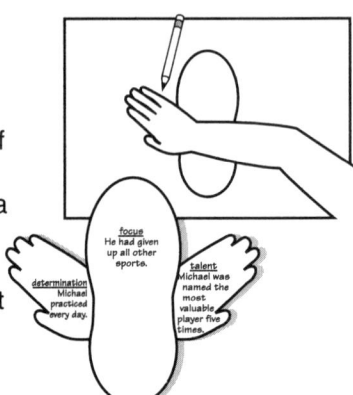

3 Supporting Details

Students will have a ball reading for details with this partner game! After reading the selection, provide each twosome with a die, a copy of page 5, and an enlarged copy of the answer key on page 79. Review the game directions below and watch students slam-dunk details!

Directions for two players:
1. Player 1 rolls the die. He finds a matching numbered statement on the net and reads it aloud. He then locates and reads the selection sentence that supports the statement.
2. Player 2 uses the letter code to check his opponent's answer on the key. If the answer is listed, Player 1 writes his initials on the line. If it is incorrect, Player 2 writes "Foul" on the line.
3. Player 2 takes his turn.
4. Players take turns until all the spaces are filled. If no unused spaces remain for a number shown on the die, the player's turn is over. The player who initials more spaces wins the game.

4 Sequence of Events

Create an over-the-top timeline that shows the sequence of events in Michael Jordan's life. As a class, have students scan the selection for several events in Jordan's life that helped lead to his success as a basketball superstar. Give each student a 12" x 18" sheet of light-colored construction paper, scissors, and glue. Then have the student complete the activity on page 6 as directed. Display the finished projects on a bulletin board titled "Jordan's Flight to Fame."

5 Cause and Effect

Take students to new heights with finding cause-and-effect relationships. Ask students to predict what will happen if you drop a basketball. *(It will bounce.)* Point out that dropping the ball is the *cause* and the bounce of the ball is the *effect.* Have students identify other cause-and-effect relationships related to basketball. (For example, if a player shoots the ball through the hoop, her team will score.) Follow up by having each student complete the activity on page 7 as directed.

Name_____ Supporting details

Slam-Dunking Details

Listen to the directions your teacher shares with you to help you complete the activity below. You'll be slam-dunking details about Michael Jordan in no time!

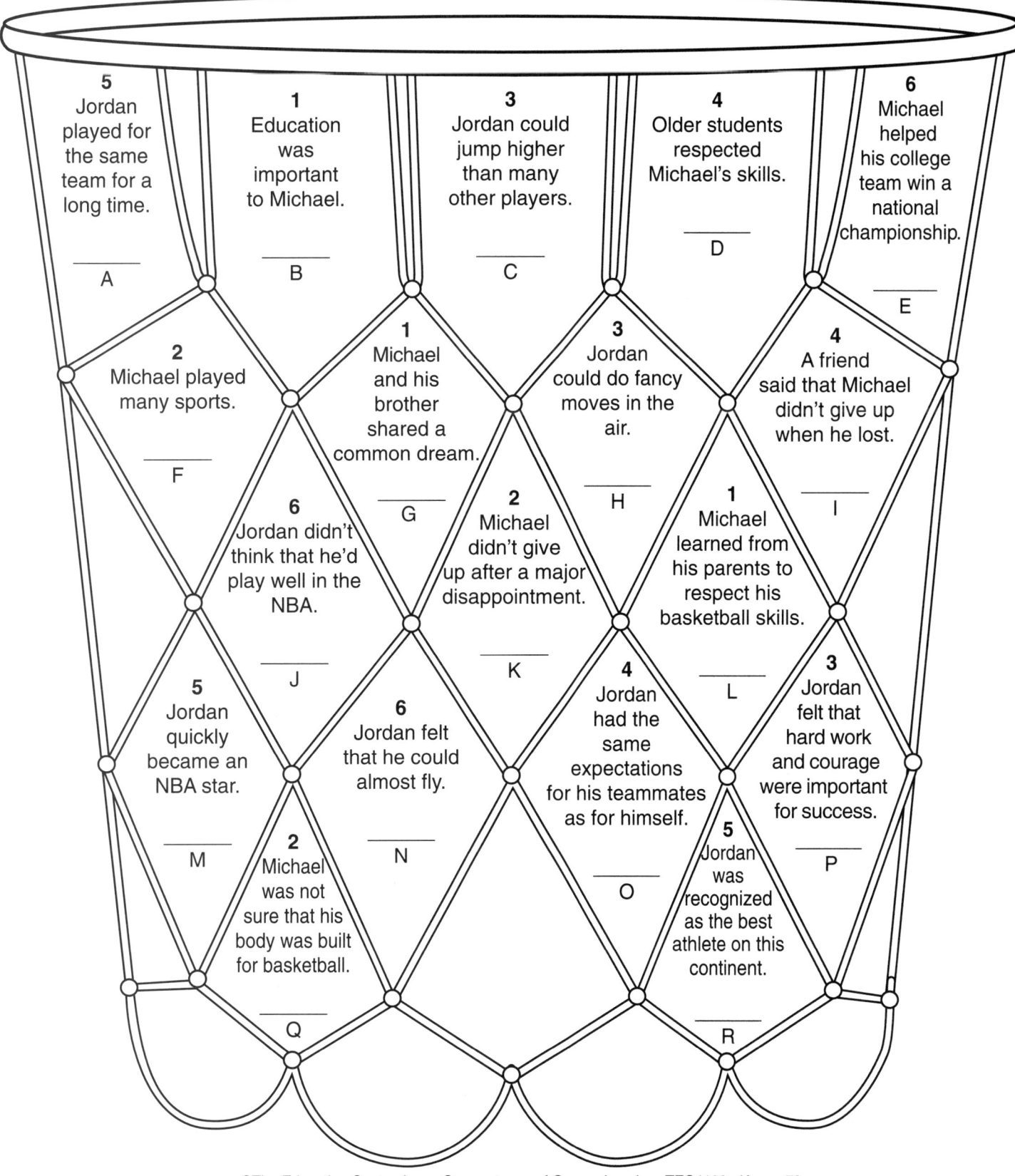

©The Education Center, Inc. • *Cornerstones of Comprehension* • TEC4103 • Key p. 79

Note to the teacher: Use with activity 3 on page 4.

Name_____   Sequence of events

Over-the-Top Timeline

Shoot to win with sequencing events on a timeline!

Directions:
1. Scan the selection and identify seven major events in Michael Jordan's life. Write the events in order in the boxes provided. The first one has been done for you.
2. Cut out the boxes along the bold lines.
3. Draw a basketball goal on a sheet of construction paper as shown.
4. Arrange the events in order from the earliest to the most recent. Then glue them in order as shown.

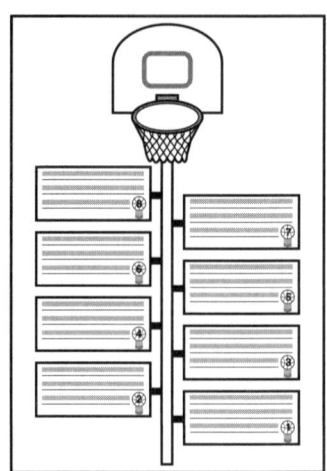

Michael and Larry practiced every day. ①

②

③

④

⑤

⑥

⑦

⑧

©The Education Center, Inc. • *Cornerstones of Comprehension* • TEC4103 • Key p. 79

6 **Note to the teacher:** Use with activity 4 on page 4.

Name _____

Cause and effect

Champion Cause and Effect

Michael Jordan has been successful both on and off the court. Follow the directions to show the cause-and-effect relationships related to his success.

Directions: Read the cause-and-effect statements on the balls below. Using a ruler, connect (between the points) Ball 1 to the ball showing its matching effect. The line will pass through two letters. Write the letters in order on the cards held by Cheerleader 1. Connect Balls 2–5 and fill in the letters in the same manner. At the end, the cheer for Jordan's college team will be revealed.

Cause

1. Michael's parents told their children not to waste their talent.
2. Jordan demanded the best of himself and his teammates.
3. Michael didn't make the varsity team his sophomore year.
4. Michael became the star player on the junior varsity team.
5. Jordan always worked hard at basketball.

Effect

- The Bulls won six championships.
- Varsity players came to the games to check out Michael's moves.
- Michael and Larry practiced every day.
- Jordan was named the greatest North American athlete of the 20th century.
- Michael's disappointment made him work even harder.

Letters on court: G R L O S H E T A E

Note to the teacher: Use with activity 5 on page 4.

7

The Barefoot Boy From Brazil

People all over the world love sports. Baseball, basketball, and football are some of the favorites in the United States. Fans watch sports on television. They support teams and cheer at **championship** games. Around the world, fans go crazy about another game—soccer. It is the most popular sport in the world. Every four years, soccer fans flock to the World Cup **tournament.** It is the sport's most famous and important event. This event isn't just a **national** contest like the Super Bowl or World Series. The winner of the World Cup becomes the champion of the whole world!

In soccer, the team as a whole is more important than any one of its players. Even so, a player often stands out. One such player was known as Pelé (pay-LAY). Pelé was born in 1940. His poor family lived in a small town in Brazil. Pelé's real name was Edson. He was named after Thomas Edison, the famous American inventor. He was nicknamed Pelé when he was about eight years old. The name stuck with him all of his life.

Pelé's father was a **professional** soccer player. Unlike professional athletes in America today, he made very little money. Pelé's mother did not want her son to play soccer. She thought it would bring him only sadness and **poverty.** Despite his mother's fears, Pelé wanted to play.

Children don't need much to play soccer. They just need a ball and a pair of shoes. Pelé did not even have those. He and his friends kicked around a sock stuffed with rags. They played in their bare feet. In their neighborhood, they were called "the **barefooted** ones." Even without shoes, Pelé became the best player in his neighborhood.

One of Brazil's best soccer players noticed Pelé's talent. He helped 15-year-old Pelé get his start in professional soccer. After playing barefoot in the street, Pelé thought it would be easy for him to win on grass-covered fields. He was right. Before long he had become the top scorer in his league. Pelé was just 17 years old when he was picked for Brazil's national team.

The team went to the World Cup tournament in 1958. Pelé was the youngest player on the field. His knee was sore and swollen from an injury. Pelé thought his coach should find a player to replace him. He asked to be sent back home. Instead, the coach put his name in the starting lineup for the third game. Pelé was about to dazzle the world with his **incredible** talent.

Goals can be rare in soccer, but Pelé scored stunning goals against the best teams in the world. In the game against France, he pulled off a *hat trick,* three goals in one game. That got the world's attention! In the game against Wales, he knocked the ball over his own head to score a goal. The world kept watching. The last game was against Sweden. Pelé juggled the ball on his instep. Then he flicked it over the goalie's head. Pelé's team won the World Cup.

Pelé and his teammates were greeted like heroes when they got back to Brazil. Their success was celebrated for months. They traveled from city to city. Everywhere the team went, the players were showered with flowers and **confetti.** They smiled so much that their cheeks hurt!

Pelé was a star on the soccer stage for more than 20 years. He was known for crazy, **acrobatic** moves. During his career, Pelé scored 1,281 goals in 1,363 games. No one has been able to break this record. The barefoot boy from Brazil had grown to be one of the greatest stars soccer has ever known.

The Barefoot Boy From Brazil

Activities

1 Vocabulary

Introduce selection vocabulary with this group activity. Ahead of time, cut out nine large hexagons from white construction paper. Label each hexagon with one boldfaced selection word. Show each word to the class as you read it aloud. Divide students into nine groups and provide each group with one paper hexagon. Instruct each group to brainstorm six terms that relate to its assigned word and to write the terms along the six edges of the hexagon. Then have group members collaborate to write a definition for the word on the back of the hexagon. Provide time for each group to present its word and related terms to the class. Follow up by having each student complete page 10 as directed.

2 Compare and Contrast

Help students identify that the author of the selection compares and contrasts information to guide their understanding of it. Begin by explaining that *comparisons* show how things are similar, while *contrasts* show how things are different. Tell students that clue words—such as *like, unlike, but, instead,* and *on the other hand*—are sometimes used to help the reader focus on similarities and differences. Have students scan the selection for clue words and identify information that is compared and contrasted. Guide students to write their own compare and contrast sentences with information found in the selection. See the example shown.

Example: Unlike the winner of the Super Bowl, the winner of the World Cup becomes champion of the world.

3 Visualization

To increase enjoyment and understanding of the selection, ask students to close their eyes and visualize as you read aloud the seventh and eighth paragraphs. Have each student make notes about the colors, sounds, and feelings he experienced as he listened. Then give each student a blank 5" x 7" index card. Instruct him to pretend to be Pelé and write a postcard to his family, describing his experience at the World Cup and the welcome-home festivities. Remind each student to make his writing both descriptive and accurate. On the other side of the index card, have the student illustrate his writing. Provide time for small groups of students to share their completed postcards.

4 Drawing Conclusions

Explain that authors sometimes convey messages to readers without saying things directly. Instead, the reader is given clues that she combines with her own experiences, and common sense to draw conclusions. Read the following statement to the class: Children don't need much to play soccer—just a ball and a pair of shoes. Point out that a conclusion could be drawn that more equipment is needed to play sports other than soccer. Invite students to brainstorm a list of several sports and equipment needed for play (for example, golf—clubs, tees, golf balls). Follow up by having each student complete the activity on page 11 as directed.

5 Main Idea and Supporting Details

Create champions at identifying main idea and supporting details with this activity! Ahead of time, draw a large trophy cup on yellow bulletin board paper and cut it out. Remind students that the main idea of a selection is its central theme and that details in the selection support the main idea. Have students brainstorm a few possible main ideas for the selection. List responses on the chalkboard. Guide students to recognize the main idea *(Pelé became one of the greatest soccer players in the world)*. Write it on the trophy cup. Then have students scan the selection to find details that support the main idea. Write the responses on the cup. Finally, have each student use the information to write a paragraph explaining how Pelé became one of the greatest soccer players in the world.

Name _____ *Vocabulary*

Vocabulary Acrobatics

Pelé was known for his amazing acrobatic moves and ability to score goals. Do a little of your own acrobatics with this vocabulary challenge!

Part 1: Read each definition below. Use the syllables shown between the goals to help identify the correct word. Mark an "X" through each one after you use it. Use the selection or a dictionary if you need help. The first one has been done for you. *(Hints: Each syllable is used once. The number of syllables for each answer is shown in parentheses.)*

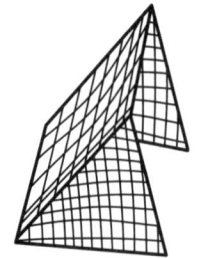

in	fes	b̶a̶t	ment	na	cham	ath	al
a̶c̶	tour	fet	lete	ship	pro	ti	bare
i	er	sion	al	ty	cred	on	i̶c̶
pov	foot	t̶i̶	ble	tion	na	pi	con

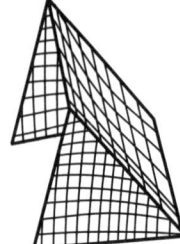

1. quickly changing position using skillful control of the body (4) a c r o b a t i c

2. lack of money and material goods (3) __ __ __ Ⓞ __ __
      7

3. a contest in which a number of players or teams take part (3) __ Ⓞ __ __ __ Ⓞ __
      3   2

4. belonging to a country (3) __ __ Ⓞ __ __ __
      1

5. a person who is skilled in or is good at physical activities that require strength, speed, or agility (2) __ __ Ⓞ __ __ __
      4

6. a contest to determine the best team (4) __ __ __ __ Ⓞ __ __ __ __ __ __
      11

7. not very believable; amazing (4) __ __ __ __ __ Ⓞ __ Ⓞ __
      13   10

8. making money for doing something that other people do for pleasure or as a hobby (4) __ Ⓞ __ __ __ Ⓞ __ __ __ __ __
      6   8

9. small pieces of paper tossed at parades or parties (3) Ⓞ __ __ __ Ⓞ __ __
      5   12

10. without shoes or other covering on the feet (2) __ __ __ Ⓞ __ __
      9

Part 2: Write the circled letters from your answers on the corresponding lines below to learn another interesting fact about Pelé.

Pelé is the only soccer player in history who has won

__ __ __ __ __   W __ __ __ __   __ __ __ __ !
12 4 7 2 9   1 6 10 13   5 3 11 8

©The Education Center, Inc. • *Cornerstones of Comprehension* • TEC4103 • Key p. 79

Note to the teacher: Use with activity 1 on page 9.

Name _____ *Drawing conclusions*

All-Star Conclusions

Part 1: Read the statements and the conclusions below. Choose two conclusions for each statement that further explain the author's message. Circle the stars next to the answers you choose.

1. Fans around the world go crazy for another sport—soccer.
   ☆ a. In other countries, many sports fans prefer soccer to football, basketball, and baseball.
   ☆ b. Many soccer fans wish they could attend the World Cup tournament.
   ☆ c. Soccer should be the most popular sport in the United States.

2. Even without shoes, Pelé was the best soccer player in his neighborhood.
   ☆ a. Pelé played a lot of soccer with his friends.
   ☆ b. He earned money to buy shoes by playing soccer.
   ☆ c. Pelé had a natural talent for playing soccer.

3. Pelé thought it would be easy to win on grass-covered fields.
   ☆ a. He thought that he would have a hard time trying to control the ball on grass.
   ☆ b. He thought he would have better control of a ball on grass than on the street.
   ☆ c. He thought he might play better if he didn't have to worry about hurting his feet.

4. In the game against France, Pelé pulled off a *hat trick*.
   ☆ a. Pelé scored more than the usual number of goals in the game against France.
   ☆ b. He took off his cap and waved it at the cheering crowd.
   ☆ c. He was so skilled at soccer that he made three goals in one game.

Part 2: Draw your own conclusions based on the details given below. Write your answers in complete sentences on the lines provided.

1. Pelé was just 17 years old when he was picked for Brazil's national team. _____
   _____

2. Pelé thought his coach should replace him on the team because his knee was sore and swollen. _____
   _____

3. In the game against Sweden, Pelé juggled the ball on his instep. Then he flicked it over the goalie's head to score a goal. Pelé's team won the World Cup. _____
   _____

4. Everywhere the team went, the players were showered with flowers and confetti. _____
   _____

Cool Connection: Why do you think that people are interested in great athletes like Pelé? Write your answer on the back of this sheet.

©The Education Center, Inc. • *Cornerstones of Comprehension* • TEC4103 • Key p. 79

Little Miss Moffitt

Little Miss Muffet might have sat on a **tuffet,** but Billie Jean Moffitt did not sit around. Even when she was about five or six years old, she knew she wanted to be the best at something. Before long she decided that she wanted to play baseball. Then she learned that girls could not play on **professional** baseball teams. So Billie Jean turned to tennis.

"What else could a little girl do if she wasn't afraid to sweat?" she said.

In the 1950s, when Billie Jean was a young girl, tennis was played at country clubs. Country clubs were for rich families. Billie Jean's father was a firefighter. They didn't have money for tennis rackets and tennis dresses. So Billie Jean played with a dime-store **racket.** She wore a shirt and shorts. She followed her town's tennis **pro** from park to park to get free lessons.

"I want to play tennis forever," she told her mother. "I'm going to be number one in the world."

Billie Jean did not seem like a girl who might become a number one tennis player. She wore big plastic glasses. She had pudgy legs. Breathing problems made her huff and puff as she played. She talked to herself on the court. She even **whooped** when she won! Before Billie Jean began to play, tennis was a quiet sport. She woke it up.

Billie Jean was one of the ten best women players in the world by the time she was 17 years old. Still, she wasn't making any money playing tennis. Women players were paid as little as ten percent of what the men earned. When Billie Jean beat the world's best female tennis player, her prize was a silver plate and six candy bars that were left on her bed by friends. Billie Jean began to ask for fair pay. She **urged** other women players to demand fair pay too. After much hard work, Billie Jean became the first female **athlete** to earn $100,000 in a year.

Billie Jean wanted interest in professional women's tennis to grow. She worked hard for equal pay and equal treatment for women tennis players. The event that most helped her cause was a tennis match against Bobby Riggs. Bobby was a former men's champion. He wanted to prove that women didn't have a place in professional tennis.

Billie Jean did not really want to play against him. Riggs had nothing to lose. Billie Jean had a lot to prove. The match was set to take place on September 20, 1973, in the Houston Astrodome. There was a lot of **publicity** ahead of time. Most people thought that Riggs would win. Over 30,000 people came to watch. Another 40 million Americans watched the match on television.

Billie Jean was upset that most of her friends thought she would lose the match. Soon after they began to play, Billie Jean was amazed to find that Bobby was a weak **foe.** She defeated him easily. She had always wanted mobs of people to cheer for tennis. Now her dream had come true. The match between Billie Jean and Bobby Riggs helped build the **popularity** of tennis. Billie Jean said, "On that night, the game of tennis finally got kicked out of the country clubs forever and into the world of real sports." All because Little Miss Moffitt, as Billie Jean was sometimes known, didn't sit on a tuffet. She went out into the world of tennis and played like a champion.

Little Miss Moffitt Activities

1 Prior Knowledge

Before reading, invite students to share their prior knowledge of tennis. Gather a tennis ball and a sheet of green bulletin board paper. Write "tennis" in the center of the paper and draw four large circles around it. Label each circle with one of the following topics: equipment and clothing, playing and scoring, tournaments, and famous players. Next, toss the ball to a student and ask her to share something she knows about tennis. Record her response under the corresponding topic. Then have the student toss the ball to a classmate and invite that student to share something he knows about the sport. Continue in the same manner until several facts have been listed for each topic. After reading the selection, review the chart with students and discuss ways it helped them understand the selection.

2 Analogies

Serve students some tennis-related analogies to build vocabulary skills. In advance, draw a tennis racket, tennis ball, hockey stick, and hockey puck, each on a separate index card. Display the cards and ask students to identify relationships among them. Guide students to understand that the relationship of the tennis racket and the tennis ball is like that of the hockey stick and the hockey puck. Invite a student to arrange the cards to show the relationship. Explain that the relationship can be expressed as an analogy, a likeness between two things that are otherwise unlike one another. Invite students to think of other analogies, such as tennis : court :: football : field. Follow up by having each student complete the activity on page 14 as directed.

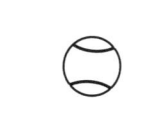

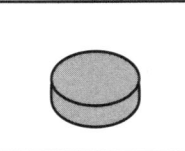

3 Character

Help students recognize that Billie Jean's words reflect some of her character traits and qualities. Provide each student with a 9" x 12" sheet of tagboard, a five-inch square of aluminum foil, scissors, and access to a glue stick and permanent marker. Direct the student to draw a handheld mirror shape (like a tennis racket) on the tagboard and cut out. Then have him cut an oval from the foil. Instruct the student to glue the oval onto the racket. Next, direct him to copy one quote from the selection on the back of the mirror. Finally, have the student use a marker to list traits or qualities that he thinks are reflected by Billie Jean's words on the front of the mirror. Display the mirrors on a bulletin board titled "Reflections of Billie Jean's Character."

4 Generalizations

Introduce students to making generalizations with this warm-up activity. Begin by writing the following statements on the chalkboard:
- The first tennis rackets had coarse, loose webbing.
- The first metal rackets were strung with piano wire, which quickly wore down tennis balls.
- These earlier rackets made playing tennis more difficult than it is today.

Invite student volunteers to read the sentences aloud. Explain that the first two are based on fact and can be proven. Then point out that the third sentence is a generalization, a broad statement or conclusion, based on the facts. Follow up by having each student complete the activity on page 15 as directed.

5 Summarizing

Challenge each student to write a summary of Billie Jean's life up to the time she defeated Bobby Riggs. Begin by leading the class in a discussion of the important events mentioned in the selection. Invite students to pretend that a biography of Billie Jean King is about to be published. Direct each student to write a brief summary of the tennis star's life for the back cover of the book. If desired, provide each student with a sheet of drawing paper, crayons, and markers. Instruct her to fold the paper in half and position it so the fold is at the left. Then have her create a colorful book cover with a picture of Billie Jean on the front and her summary on the back.

Analogy Athletics

The secret of success with analogies is to identify the relationship between the word pairs. Study the examples below, which show five different kinds of analogies. **Hint:** : = *is to* and :: = *as*.

Examples:
- a. *correct* : *true* :: *incorrect* : *false* (synonyms)
- b. *north* : *south* :: *east* : *west* (antonyms)
- c. *song* : *sing* :: *ad* : *advertisement* (word form changes, such as from a noun to a verb)
- d. *student* : *class* :: *drummer* : *band* (member/group)
- e. *scissors* : *cut* :: *pen* : *write* (object/use)

Directions: Read each analogy and think about the relationship between the two words given. Choose an example from above that shows the same kind of relationship. Write the letter on the tennis ball. Then complete the analogy using a word from the list. The first one has been done for you.

(C) 1. difficult : difficulty :: public : __publicity__

(   ) 2. actress : movie :: _____ : sport

(   ) 3. _____ : whisper :: loud : soft

(   ) 4. _____ : metal :: oak : wood

(   ) 5. baseball glove : _____ :: tennis racket : swing

(   ) 6. friend : _____ :: rich : poor

(   ) 7. bed : sleep :: _____ : sit

(   ) 8. popular : _____ :: similar : similarity

(   ) 9. beginner : amateur :: expert : _____

(   ) 10. gain : lose :: _____ : spend

(   ) 11. _____ : professional :: doc : doctor

(   ) 12. _____ : encourage :: ask : request

Word Bank
foe
popularity
whoop
silver
pro
athlete
publicity
tuffet
earn
professional
urge
catch

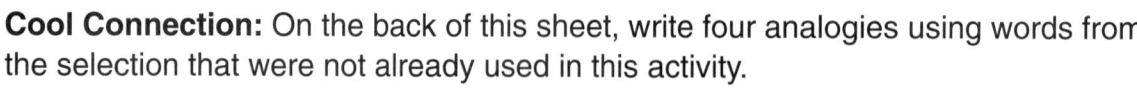

Cool Connection: On the back of this sheet, write four analogies using words from the selection that were not already used in this activity.

Name _____

Generalizations

Tennis, Generally Speaking

Part 1: Read the facts and generalizations below. Then, on the lines provided, write one or more additional facts that support each generalization. Remember: A generalization is a broad statement based on facts.

Part 2: Make your own generalizations based on the facts given below. Write your answers on the lines provided.

a. Billie Jean was one of the ten best women players by the time she was 17.
b. She defeated the world's best female tennis player.
   Generalization: _____

a. Bobby Riggs had nothing to lose.
b. Billie Jean had a lot to prove.
G Generalization: _____

a. More than 30,000 people watched the match in the Houston Astrodome.
b. Another 40 million Americans watched it on television.
   Generalization: _____

a. Billie Jean's father was a firefighter.
b. _____

Generalization: Billie Jean's family wasn't wealthy.

a. Billie Jean wore big plastic glasses.
b. _____

Generalization: Billie Jean didn't look like a typical tennis player.

a. _____
b. _____

Generalization: Billie Jean didn't act like most tennis players.

Cool Connection: Copy a set of two or three facts from the selection on the back of this sheet. Then write a generalization based on those facts.

15

Note to the teacher: Use with activity 4 on page 13.

A Boy Called Curly

Crazy Horse grew up on the Great Plains. He was a serious, quiet child. People called him Curly because he had soft, curly hair. Curly's father was a **prophet.** He was respected for his wisdom and good advice. He also loved his son. Curly would sit on his father's shoulders and grab each of his braids. His father would prance around the tipi like a horse as Curly screamed with delight.

Like other Sioux boys of 13, Curly left home to seek a **vision.** He **fasted,** going without food for two days. He grew tired. No vision came until the third day. He saw a man on a horse float toward him. The horseman wore no paint. He wore a hawk's feather in his hair. He had a brown stone tied behind one ear. Arrows and bullets flew toward the horseman. They fell away without touching him. Then Curly saw the horseman's own people grabbing his arms. They tried to hold him back. The horseman shook them off. What could the vision mean for Curly?

Even though the rider didn't speak, Curly understood his message. The vision showed Curly how to dress for battle. He also learned that he must never take anything for himself after a fight. Later, Curly told his father about the vision. His father told Curly that he should trust his vision. He said that Curly would never be hurt in battle if he dressed and acted like the horseman. He must stand up to danger, even when his people tried to hold him back.

Curly was soon ready for his first battle. He wanted to be brave. He fought **fearlessly** against an enemy tribe. He rode safely through danger just as his vision showed him. Curly was too **modest** to brag about his bravery when he returned home. But his father wasn't! He proudly gave his son a new name—Crazy Horse.

As a young **warrior,** Crazy Horse was chosen to be a **shirt-wearer.** This meant that it was his duty to protect the people. The four shirt-wearers made sure people respected the rights of everyone in the tribe. Crazy Horse was chosen for both his courage and his kindness. He loved to tell stories to children. He enjoyed teaching the young boys in the village the skills they would need as adults. He was known for his **charity.** He often gave fresh meat to the poor. He always remembered his vision and since his first battle, never took anything for himself after a battle.

The Sioux worried as more white American settlers moved west. The Americans wanted to take over their land. The United States government tried to force Native Americans to live on special **reservations.** Crazy Horse refused to move from his native land. He led his people in fights against white forces.

After several years of **resisting** the settlers, Crazy Horse grew tired of running. He did not want to give up his freedom. He did not want to surrender to an army that had never beaten him in battle. But he saw the suffering of his people. Crazy Horse decided to give in. He agreed to live on an Indian reservation. Soon after moving there, Crazy Horse died. A guard killed him as an Indian policeman held his arms. Crazy Horse's vision had come true. One of his own people had held his arms as he was killed.

Before his surrender, Crazy Horse seemed to have a feeling that he would not live much longer. Perhaps he wondered how he could help protect his people when he was gone. His people escaped to freedom after he died. The soldiers did not even try to stop them. They watched as the people disappeared into the hills. Even after his death, Crazy Horse led his people to freedom. His spirit was with them.

A Boy Called Curly

Activities

1 Context Clues

Crazy Horse's vision guided him throughout his life. Show young readers that context clues can guide them through reading a selection filled with challenging vocabulary. Remind students that *context clues* are the words or phrases around an unknown word that help the reader determine its meaning. Before reading the selection, distribute a copy of page 18 to each student. Discuss the three different types of context clues described on the page. As a class, have students brainstorm their own examples. Then provide each student with a red, blue, and green colored pencil and instruct him to complete the activity on page 18 as directed.

2 Author's Purpose

Remind students that the author's purpose in writing the selection may be to inform, entertain, or persuade. Provide each student with a six-inch feather cut out of construction paper. Then have students number the selection paragraphs and count off from 1 to 8. Direct each student to reread the paragraph that corresponds with his number and then write one detail about Crazy Horse's life on his feather cutout. Invite students to share their details. Next, guide students in determining what type of information their details contained *(facts)* to figure out the author's purpose *(to inform the reader about Crazy Horse's life)*. Write the purpose on a 3" x 14" paper strip using a black marker. Tape the strip to an area of your classroom. Invite students to add their feathers to create an informative headdress display.

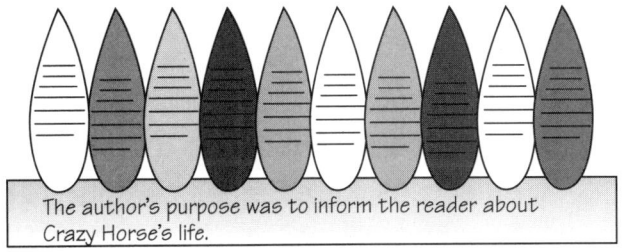

The author's purpose was to inform the reader about Crazy Horse's life.

3 Predictions

Plains Indians sometimes decorated tipis with designs seen in a vision. Have students decorate their own tipis with predictions related to Curly's vision. Provide each student with half of a brown paper grocery bag. Have her cut a large half oval from the bag as shown. Direct the student to read the first three paragraphs of the selection. Instruct her to write a sentence that describes one detail about the vision on the bag and then illustrate her sentence. Then have her write a prediction about a possible meaning for Curly beneath her drawing. Finally, have each student overlap and glue the oval's edges to create the tipi. After reading the selection, have students share their work and compare their predictions.

4 Character

The selection tells us that Crazy Horse was both a fierce warrior and a compassionate leader. Remind students that readers determine a character's traits by identifying the character's actions, feelings, and thoughts. Give the following example: Crazy Horse often gave fresh meat to the poor. Ask students what this action shows the reader *(Crazy Horse was kind and generous)*. Have students scan the selection for examples of actions, feelings, or thoughts that portray Crazy Horse as a fierce warrior or a compassionate leader. Follow up by having each student complete the activity on page 19 as directed.

5 Fact and Opinion

Students are likely to have strong opinions about how Native Americans were forced to leave their land. Explain to students that *facts* are provable statements. *Opinions* cannot be proven and may relate to one's beliefs. Pair students and provide each pair with eight index cards. Instruct one student in each pair to write a selection fact on a card, and her partner to write an opinion about the fact on a second card. Have the pairs take turns writing facts and opinions using the remaining cards. Provide time for each pair to share its statements with the class. To provide further practice with fact and opinion, place the cards at a center for students to sort.

Name_____   Context clues

Seeking Context Clues

Directions: Study the examples of the three types of context clues. Then read the story and think about each boldfaced word. Underline the words that give clues about its meaning. Decide which type of context clue was used and circle the boldfaced word with the corresponding color.

Red = comparison or contrast clue:
The little boy was frightened, but his older sister was *brave*.

Blue = synonym clue:
The supply of buffalo meat was *abundant*. There was plenty.

Green = definition clue:
The *shaman*, or holy man, cured the sick warrior.

Little Eagle lived with his family in the wide open plains. His father was a **prophet.** He could predict the future. The U.S. government wanted Little Eagle's family to move to a **reservation,** special land set aside for Native Americans. Little Eagle's parents spent many years **resisting** them. They would not give in.

Little Eagle loved to hunt. His brothers were **modest** about their hunting skills. Little Eagle was a show-off. When he was 11, he set out on a buffalo hunt. He rode **fearlessly** into a herd of buffalo. He acted bravely. Before he knew what was happening, a bull turned around and jumped at his pony. Little Eagle fell to the ground with a thud. He was almost trampled to death! After many days of rest, Little Eagle **fasted,** hoping to overcome his shame. He went without food for many days. He decided that the life of a hunter was not for him. He did not want to become a **warrior.** He wanted to be a peacemaker. Little Eagle spent the rest of his life helping people. He became known for his **charity,** or kindness toward the poor.

Cool Connection: Think about the three kinds of context clues. Then write a sentence for each word listed below using a different context clue. Write your sentences on the back of this sheet. Use a dictionary if you need help.

brave   vision   shame

Name _____ Character

Putting on Character Traits

Many people think of Crazy Horse as a fierce warrior. The selection tells us that he was a kind, peaceful man as well.

Directions: Study the character traits listed in the box. List the traits that describe Crazy Horse during peace on the left. List the traits that describe him during war on the right. Use a dictionary if you need help. Support your answer by writing an event from the selection in which Crazy Horse shows that trait. The first one has been done for you.

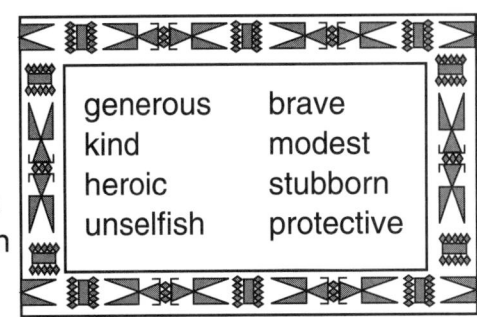

generous   brave
kind   modest
heroic   stubborn
unselfish protective

Crazy Horse During Peace

generous : He often gave fresh meat to the poor.

Crazy Horse During War

©The Education Center, Inc. • Cornerstones of Comprehension • TEC4103 • Key p. 79

Note to the teacher: Use with activity 4 on page 17.

The Furry Friends of Billy Moon

The shy little boy with hair that curled beneath his ears grew up in England. Like many other wealthy English children of the 1920s, a **nanny** cared for him most of the day. The boy enjoyed spending time with his father. They went for long walks through acres of woods and looked for birds' nests. They solved math problems and crossword puzzles. The boy's father nicknamed him "Billy Moon." Most of the time, he simply called the little boy "Moon."

Moon had a zoo of stuffed animals. There was a tiny pig with a round belly. His toy tiger was as fuzzy as a peach. He had a sweet-smiling kangaroo who carried a **joey** in her pouch. He loved the rumpled old bear that he got when he was a baby. Moon's father watched and listened as his son played with his cuddly **companions** in the forest. He started writing stories about them. He added a rabbit and an owl, which were based on real forest animals. He had an **illustrator** draw pictures of Moon and his furry friends. Billy Moon was one of the main characters in his father's books.

When the books were **published,** readers loved them! By the time Moon went away to school, he was known all over the world. The illustrator had copied Moon's photo well. The boy pictured in the stories wore shoes with buckles and had long hair that curled under his ears. The boy looked just like Moon. Perhaps this was why strangers confused the real boy with the **character** from his father's stories. This may have **embarrassed** Moon. After all, he was not a storybook character. He was a real boy with his own feelings. Being famous was not all bad, though. Moon and his flock of furry friends proudly marched in a parade. He even received fan mail from folks all over the world.

Children lose, give away, or wear out their stuffed animals. Moon was no different. Over the years, his friends were loved to pieces. They were worn and torn, stitched and sewed. His baby kangaroo was lost in the woods. What happened to the rest of his furry friends? When Moon was older, his father gave them to a publisher. The publisher later **donated** them to the New York Public Library. The library put them on display in the children's room. Even though Moon no longer plays with his friends, they're never lonely. Close to a million people visit them every year!

When people come to visit the famous stuffed toys, perhaps they think about how the animals in the stories acted just like people. Eeyore's gray color matched his gloomy mood. Kanga, filled with energy, cared for her curious baby Roo. Tigger, the frisky tiger, could not sit still. Piglet was **timid** and shy. Owl was known for his wisdom. Rabbit just wanted to know everyone's business. And Pooh was the honey-loving bear who got along with them all.

If you know Winnie-the-Pooh and his friends, then you may have guessed Billy Moon's real name. It was Christopher Robin Milne. His father was A. A. Milne, the author of the famous Winnie-the-Pooh stories. So the next time you read a book or see a movie about Pooh, remember that there was a real boy behind the stories. He loved crossword puzzles, math, and the woods. And he loved his bear.

The Furry Friends of Billy Moon
Activities

1 Predictions

Phase students into making and revising predictions with this activity. Provide each student with a copy of the selection, four four-inch white paper circles and access to a stapler. Have the student stack the circles and staple them as shown. Explain that the selection is about a famous boy whose nickname was Billy Moon. As a class, read the first paragraph from the selection. Invite students to guess, or *predict,* who Billy Moon really is. Direct each student to write a prediction on his first circle. Have him continue reading, stopping after the second and third paragraphs to write a new or revised prediction on each of the next two circles. After the student has read the entire selection, check to make sure he has written Moon's real name on the last circle.

2 Vocabulary

Reinforce the meanings of valuable new vocabulary words with this activity. Remind students that one of the activities that Moon and his father enjoyed together was doing crossword puzzles. Tell students that working crossword puzzles can be an interesting, fun way to learn about word meanings. Provide each student with a copy of page 22 and a dictionary. Have each student complete the activity on the page as directed.

3 Personification

A. A. Milne used *personification* by writing about animals as though they were people. Help students learn more about personification by having them write short skits about the characters. Begin by directing students' attention to the fifth paragraph in the selection. List the animal characters from Milne's stories on the chalkboard. Invite students to use selection details to identify each animal's main character traits. Divide students into small groups. Have each group write the dialogue for a short skit about a day Pooh got stuck in the door of Rabbit's house. For each character, have students include at least one line of dialogue that accurately reflects the character's traits. If desired, provide time for each group to perform its skit.

4 Imagery

Use this creative project to remind students that imagery expresses ideas vividly and adds interest to reading selections. As a class, scan the selection for examples of imagery, such as "Moon and his flock of furry friends proudly marched in a parade." Discuss the responses. Next, provide each student with a 16-inch length of adding machine paper, a 4" x 6" index card, scissors, clear tape, and crayons or markers. Direct the student to divide the paper into four four-inch sections. In each section, have him write and illustrate one sentence from the selection that produces a picture in his mind. To complete the project, direct the student to carefully cut two slits in the card as shown. Then have him insert the paper through both slots and tape the ends, forming a loop. Provide time for each student to share his parade of images with the class.

5 Drawing Conclusions

Explain to students that an author sometimes conveys a message to his readers without saying it directly. The author gives the reader clues in the form of statements or facts. The reader uses the information and his own experience and common sense to draw a conclusion. Invite a student volunteer to read the first paragraph. Point out that the reader might draw the conclusion that Billy Moon had no brothers or sisters. Ask students to identify the information that would support this conclusion. *(A nanny cared for Moon. He spent time with his father. There is no mention of another child participating in these activities.)* Follow up by having each student complete the activity on page 23 as directed.

Name _____   *Vocabulary*

Christopher Robin's Crossword Connection

Part 1: Read each definition. Then use the words from the word bank to complete the puzzle. Use a dictionary if you need help.

Word Bank
donate   nanny
publish   joey
companion   character
timid   illustrator
embarrass   buckle

Across
3 a person who keeps another person company
4 an artist who draws pictures for books or magazines
7 to give money or other belongings to a fund or cause
9 a clasp used to fasten one end of a belt to the other
10 to print a book or other item and offer it for sale

Down
1 a person who works for a family by taking care of the children
2 to cause someone to feel nervous or ill at ease
5 a baby kangaroo
6 a person or figure in a story, book, play, or movie
8 shy or easily frightened

Part 2: The author of the Winnie-the-Pooh stories was A. A. Milne. To find out what the initials stand for, locate the letters shown inside the special symbols on the puzzle. Then write the letters on the lines with the matching symbols.

__ __ __ __   __ __ __   X   __ __ __ __ __
○ △ ○ □   ○ △ ◇   ○ □ ☆ ◇ ▽

©The Education Center, Inc. • *Cornerstones of Comprehension* • TEC4103 • Key p. 79

Note to the teacher: Use with activity 2 on page 21.

Name _____   *Drawing conclusions*

What's the Message?

Part 1: Read the following statements. Choose the best conclusion based on these statements and the information given in the selection. Color the book next to your answer.

1. Moon and his father went for long walks. They looked for birds' nests. They did math problems and crossword puzzles together.
   - a. Moon didn't know his father very well.
   - b. Moon enjoyed doing things with his father.
   - c. Moon liked to spend time outdoors.

2. Moon was a shy little boy. He had a zoo of stuffed animals.
   - a. Moon wanted to be a zookeeper when he grew up.
   - b. Moon didn't have any toy cars or trucks.
   - c. Moon was a quiet child whose stuffed animals were like friends.

3. Moon's father watched and listened as his son played with his stuffed animals. He began writing stories about them.
   - a. Moon's father was a writer who didn't have any ideas for books.
   - b. Moon's father thought that people might enjoy reading about the games Moon played with his furry friends.
   - c. Moon's father thought his son shouldn't play with stuffed animals.

4. Moon's father had an illustrator draw pictures of Moon and his furry friends for the books.
   - a. Moon's father thought his son would make a good character for the books.
   - b. Moon's father only liked to draw pictures of tigers, bears, pigs, and kangaroos.
   - c. The illustrator watched Moon play and then drew the pictures.

Part 2: Draw your own conclusions based on the details given below. Write each answer in a complete sentence on the lines provided.

1. Some people confused Moon with the character from his father's stories. This may have embarrassed the real boy. _____

2. Moon received lots of fan mail, and he marched in a parade with his furry friends. _____

3. Moon loved his furry friends to pieces. They were worn and torn, stitched and sewed. _____

4. When Moon was older, his father gave the stuffed animals to a publisher. The publisher gave them to the New York Public Library. _____

©The Education Center, Inc. • *Cornerstones of Comprehension* • TEC4103 • Key p. 79

A Notebook in His Pocket, Liberty on His Mind

Study, study, study. That's all the young man with red hair and freckles seemed to do. Early each morning, Thomas poked his nose into his science books. After breakfast, he turned his quick mind to **politics.** History made a tasty afternoon snack. He spooned down a few more subjects before going to sleep each night.

Thomas Jefferson was born in 1743. He grew up on a tobacco **plantation** in Virginia. Tom worked hard on the farm. In his spare time, he liked to swim, fish, and ride fast horses. He also loved to spend time with his father.

Tom's father wanted his son to have a good education. Tom learned to read and write when he was very young. By the time he was six, he had read all of his father's books. He wrote in small, neat letters using sharp **quill** pens. He got in the habit of writing his thoughts in notebooks that he kept in his pockets. He felt that they helped him keep his life in order.

As a young man, Jefferson went to college in Williamsburg, Virginia. His days were filled with the study of science, math, history, and languages. He worked hard and packed new ideas and thoughts into his many notebooks. After college, he chose to study law.

Jefferson kept right on using notebooks. When he started his law career, he made notes about his cases. Later, he kept notes and plans for **Monticello,** his home on the top of a mountain. He kept notebooks for accounts and lists of things to do. He even kept a garden book with lists of things he grew at Monticello.

Jefferson was also busy with politics. At that time, Virginia was one of 13 American **colonies** ruled by King George III of England. The king had begun to tax books, paint, glass, tea, and other things the colonists needed. He let soldiers search the colonists' homes. Angry colonists held a meeting, or **congress,** to decide what to do. Jefferson used his pen to voice his thoughts. He wrote to the men of the congress, saying that the king didn't have the right to rule the colonies.

This idea shocked many of the men in congress. They still hoped to find a peaceful way to solve the problems with England. Finally, it was clear that peace with the king could not be reached. Jefferson and four other men were asked to write a Declaration of Independence. It would tell the king and the rest of the world why Americans would fight for the right to **govern** themselves.

All five men expressed their ideas, but Jefferson did all of the writing. He chose each word carefully. He wrote that everyone has a right to **liberty,** or freedom. He said that all people are created equal. Even though Jefferson owned slaves, he thought slavery should end. He wrote that the king was wrong for allowing the slave trade. After 17 days of writing and rewriting, he thought the declaration was perfect.

The men in the congress argued over almost every word. One man, John Adams, fought to keep the declaration the way it had been written. In the end, there were only a few changes made to the **document.** It was a little shorter and the part about ending slavery had been taken out. It was signed on July 4, 1776. The colonies were free from England.

Jefferson went on to become our country's third president. He also **founded** the University of Virginia. Jefferson died on July 4, 1826, 50 years after his words gave birth to our country. The man who always had a notebook in his pocket had changed the world with a pen.

A Notebook in His Pocket, Liberty on His Mind

Activities

1. Vocabulary

Introduce vocabulary by having each student create her own "Words in My Pocket" booklet. Provide each student with a sheet of lined paper, scissors, and access to a stapler. Direct each student to fold the paper into thirds horizontally and cut along the folds as shown. Then have the student stack the sheets, fold them in half vertically, and staple them near the folded edge to form a booklet. Direct each student to write one boldfaced word at the top of each page. Then have her write the following below each word: the selection sentence, the word's meaning, and an original sentence. Encourage the student to use her notebook as a reference as she reads the selection.

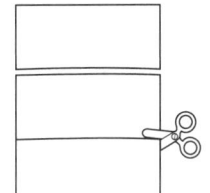

2. Cause and Effect

Help students determine cause-and-effect relationships in Jefferson's life with the following activity. Begin by explaining that an *effect* is what happens and a *cause* is why something happens. List cause-and-effect clue words on the chalkboard *(because, since, when, so, then, as a result of, therefore)*. Have students practice combining cause-and-effect statements using the clue words and the sentences shown below. Follow up by having each student complete page 26 as directed.

Examples:
- Thomas worked hard on the farm.
- In his spare time, Thomas liked to fish and swim.

(Since Thomas worked hard, he liked to fish and swim in his spare time.)

3. Main Idea and Supporting Details

Engage students in learning about main ideas and supporting details with this bulletin board display. In advance, divide each of six 9" x 12" sheets of white construction paper into four sections. Program the first section of each window with one of the main ideas listed below. Divide students into six groups and give one window to each group. Instruct each group to read its assigned main idea, scan the selection for supporting details, and record the details in the remaining window sections. Provide time for groups to share their work. If desired, display the windows on a bulletin board–sized cutout of Jefferson's home (see the illustration). Title the display "Main Ideas at Monticello."

Main Ideas:
- Jefferson was a good student.
- Jefferson used notebooks to keep track of many things.
- Jefferson used his writing to express his thoughts.
- The colonies wanted to be free from British rule.
- Jefferson believed in freedom and liberty.
- Jefferson is famous for the many things he did for our country.

4. Character

Jefferson was such an important character in history that his portrait is on the 1976-issue two-dollar bill. Have students brainstorm a list of Jefferson's character traits *(studious, intelligent, famous, etc.)*. Circulate a two-dollar bill or picture of the bill. (Pictures of the bill are available at http://www.bep.treas.gov, Keyword: collecting, and in books on U.S. currency.) Provide each student with a 4½" x 12" sheet of light green construction paper. Direct students to draw an oval-shaped portrait of Jefferson in the center. On each side of the portrait, have students write one of Jefferson's character traits and a selection detail supporting the trait. On the back, have students write a paragraph telling how his character traits made him a good choice to write the Declaration of Independence.

5. Analogies

Thomas Jefferson had a sharp mind for words. Use this activity to sharpen students' minds for analogies. Remind students that an *analogy* shows a likeness between two objects that are otherwise unlike. Copy the analogies shown on the chalkboard (without the italicized answers). Invite a student volunteer to read each one. Have her explain how the words in the first pair go together. Then direct her to identify the missing word and write it on the chalkboard. (Students may refer to the selection if they need help.) Follow up by having each student complete the activity on page 27 as directed.

Examples:
- evening : dinner :: morning : *breakfast*
- wide : narrow :: longer : *shorter*
- ten : nine :: fourth : *third*

Name _____

Cause and effect

Revolutionary Results

John Adams wanted Jefferson to write the Declaration of Independence *because* Jefferson was a better writer. In fact, Adams said, "You can write ten times better than I can." Think about the following cause-and-effect events.

Cause: Jefferson was a good writer.   **Effect:** He was asked to write an important document.

Directions: Read each cause statement shown on the left. Use the selection to help you find the matching effect on the right. Label each ink bottle with the matching letter.

1. Jefferson learned to read when he was very young.
2. Jefferson felt that writing things down helped him keep his life in order.
3. Jefferson thought that slavery was wrong.
4. Jefferson wrote to the men of the congress saying that the king had no right to rule the colonists.
5. Problems between the king and the colonists couldn't be solved.
6. The Declaration of Independence was signed on July 4, 1776.
7. The king began to tax the colonists and let his soldiers search their homes.
8. John Adams fought to keep Jefferson's words.
9. The congress did not agree with parts of the declaration.
10. Jefferson was a good writer who believed the colonies should be free.

A. Congress removed a part about slavery.
B. Congress decided to declare the colonies free from England.
C. Most of the declaration was unchanged.
D. He wrote that the king was wrong for allowing the slave trade.
E. Jefferson wrote his thoughts and ideas in notebooks.
F. Jefferson was chosen to write the Declaration of Independence.
G. Men in the congress were shocked by Jefferson's words.
H. Jefferson had read all of his father's books by the time he was six.
I. The angry colonists held a meeting to talk about problems with the king.
J. The colonies declared themselves free from British rule.

Cool Connection: On the back of this sheet, write at least two sentences telling what may have caused people to vote for Jefferson, making him the third president of the United States. Remember that a *cause* is why something happens.

Note to the teacher: Use with activity 2 on page 25.

©The Education Center, Inc. • *Cornerstones of Comprehension* • TEC4103 • Key p. 79

Name_____ *Analogies*

An Analogy in His Pocket

T. J. has a sharp mind for words, but he is having some trouble. Follow the directions below to help him solve the analogies listed on the sign.

Directions: Read the passage below. Look back at the selection to help you fill in the missing words. Then use the words you filled in to complete the analogies that follow. *(Hint: The words will not be used in the order they are found in the passage.)* One has been done for you.

Thomas Jefferson grew up on a plantation in **a.** _____. He worked hard and liked to **b.** _____ his free time swimming and fishing. He learned to read when he was very **c.** _____. Later, he studied history, math, **d.** _____, and languages. He often wrote his thoughts and ideas in **e.** _____. He wrote in small, neat **f.** _____. As a young man, Jefferson became a **g.** _____. He was busy in politics. When the colonies wanted to be free from England, he used his **h.** _____ to speak for Americans. Jefferson believed that all people were created **i.** _____. He believed that **j.** _____ was wrong. He also believed that education was important, so he **k.** *founded* the University of Virginia. Jefferson became the third **l.** _____ of the United States.

1. began : *founded* :: started : set up
2. teacher : school :: _____ : court
3. Spanish : language :: biology : _____
4. city : mayor :: country : _____
5. cut : knife :: write : _____
6. Austin : Texas :: Richmond : _____
7. child : _____ :: grandmother : old
8. doctor : charts :: student : _____
9. rich : poor :: save : _____
10. more : extra :: same : _____
11. alphabet : _____ :: musical scale : notes
12. _____ : bondage :: liberty : freedom

©The Education Center, Inc. • *Cornerstones of Comprehension* • TEC4103 • Key p. 79

Note to the teacher: Use with activity 5 on page 25.

Are You Blue?

Feeling a bit blue? Then you aren't alone in the animal kingdom. You probably can name some black, brown, and gray animals. Perhaps you can name a pink animal or one that is green. Can you think of any animals that are downright blue? Blue animals can be found around the world. They swim in the seas and soar through the skies. They scramble up trees and scamper over snowdrifts. Yet you may not even know they exist.

One rare blue animal searches for plants, fish, and fruit in southeast Alaska. Even people who live in this area may never see this **shy** beast. Like other bears, its body is heavy and strong. It has short legs and large feet that end in sharp, curved claws. Its cousins may have black, brown, or cinnamon fur, but the **glacier** bear wears a coat of a different color. A mixture of black and gray hairs gives the glacier bear its special color and its nickname, blue bear.

Another **Arctic** animal dressed in blue fur can **outfox** fish, rodents, and birds to make a tasty meal of them. To adapt to life in the far north, the Arctic fox grows the warmest fur of any animal. Its furry coat covers it from the tips of its small, round ears to the bottoms of its padded paws. The fox wraps its bushy tail around its nose when it sleeps to stay snug as a bug in a rug. The fur of the **coastal** Arctic fox changes from bluish gray or bluish black in winter to chocolate brown in the summer. Its **inland** brothers and sisters wear white with winter's snow. They all sport coats of gray-brown when summer warms the far north.

Some blue creatures wear feathers instead of fur. The great blue heron looks like the king of birds. It even wears a blue-black crown and a white crest on its head. With a **wingspan** of up to six feet, the heron looks **majestic** as it flies slowly over lakes and marshes. The heron stands about four feet tall on thin, stiltlike legs. Trying to keep its feathers dry, it wades through shallow water searching for prey. Lizards, frogs, fish, rodents, and insects are all fair game for this fowl. Few escape the sharp thrust of the heron's long yellow bill.

The crabbiest blue animal **scuttles** along the Atlantic coast. The blue crab has lots of legs, ten in all. Eight walking legs scoot it sideways in the sand. The back pair are shaped like paddles. They help whisk the crab through the water in any direction. The crab's two front legs with strong, quick claws clutch food. Small fish, oysters, and clams are some of the crab's favorite snacks. Its strange eyes stick out from stalks above its hard outer shell. When it has outgrown its shell, the crab leaves it behind. With a little luck, it won't be caught by someone looking for a tasty meal before its new shell hardens. No wonder the blue crab feels **crabby!**

The largest blue animal of all is the blue whale. It can be found in all oceans. An adult might be 100 feet long and weigh over 150 tons. That's longer and heavier than three school buses! This giant mammal's favorite food is a tiny shrimplike animal called **krill.** A blue whale has a strong tail, thin flippers, and a tube-shaped body that make it a whale of a swimmer. The blue whale has the loudest cry of any animal on Earth. Its musical calls can be heard thousands of miles away.

Whether they are shy, crabby, foxy, majestic, or musical, these animals are treasures of the animal kingdom. With blue animals in the world to enjoy, who could feel blue?

Are You Blue?

Activities

1 Prior Knowledge

Before reading the selection, preview facts about animal habitats. Ahead of time, program nine index cards, each with one of the following terms: *Arctic, inland, coastal, ocean, glacier bear, Arctic fox, great blue heron, blue crab,* and *blue whale.* Explain that the selection is about unique animals living in a variety of environments. Display the four habitat cards and invite students to share what they know about each habitat's characteristics. Then read the names of the animals and have student volunteers predict where each animal might live and why. Post each animal card beside its corresponding habitat card. Allow time for students to revise their predictions after reading the selection.

2 Supporting Details

Does identifying important details puzzle your students? Help students piece together selection details with this fun activity. After reading the selection, guide students to identify three common details given for each animal, such as geographical location, physical description, and food. Provide each student with a copy of page 30 and discuss the directions. Once the information has been completed, have students cut out, mix together, and reassemble each of their puzzles. If desired, have students swap puzzles so they have the opportunity to assemble one puzzle for each animal described in "Are You Blue?"

3 Comparing and Contrasting

Not much can compare to this three-dimensional graphic organizer! Demonstrate how to compare and contrast two chosen animals on the organizer by following the directions below:

1. Fold a nine-inch square of construction paper in half to form a triangle. Then fold it in half again.
2. Unfold the paper. Cut along one fold line, stopping at the square's center.
3. Write the name of a different animal on each of the top two triangles as shown. Write the geographical location, physical characteristics, and prey for each animal in its corresponding triangle.
4. Write at least three similarities between the two animals on a bottom triangle.
5. Draw each animal on the back of its corresponding triangle.
6. Overlap the two bottom triangles so that the writing appears on top. Glue the triangles in place.

4 Homophones

Send students on a homophone hunt through the selection to boost vocabulary skills. Remind students that *homophones* are words that sound the same but have different meanings or different spellings. Instruct each student to reread the selection and circle at least 15 words that could be homophones. Follow up by having each student complete the activity on page 31 as directed.

5 Alliteration

Introduce students to the ABCs of alliteration! Explain that *alliteration* occurs when beginning consonant sounds are repeated in words. Invite students to skim the selection to find alliterative sentences and phrases. Discuss how the author used alliteration to create word pictures in the reader's mind. Next, provide each student with a copy of page 32 and have him use the graphic organizer to help him write his own alliterative sentences. Allow time for students to share several of their sensational sentences with the class.

Name _____ *Supporting details*

A Perfect Fit

Directions: Write the names of three animals from the selection in the spaces provided. Fill in each remaining puzzle piece with details about the animal. *(Hint: The more information you write, the easier it will be to put the puzzle together.)* Cut out and mix the puzzle pieces. Then use the details you wrote to put the puzzles back together.

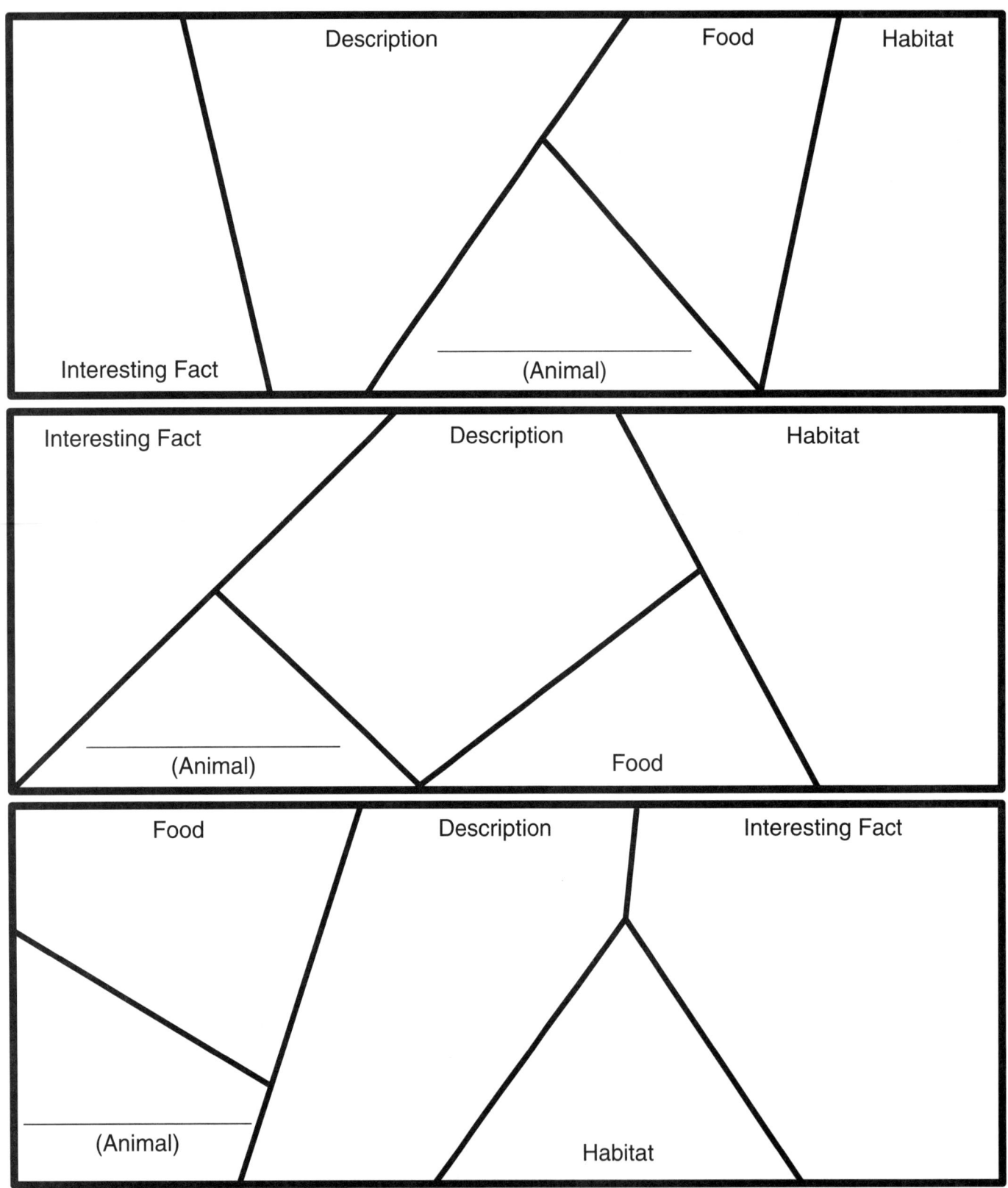

©The Education Center, Inc. • *Cornerstones of Comprehension* • TEC4103 • Key p. 79

Note to the teacher: Use with activity 2 on page 29.

Name_____ Homophones

Here, Hear!

Directions: Read each word below. Reread the selection to find its matching homophone. Write the homophone in the space provided on the animal. Then, on the lines provided, write an original sentence about each animal using as many of the listed homophones as you can.

1
- fir _____
- bare _____
- sea _____
- feat _____

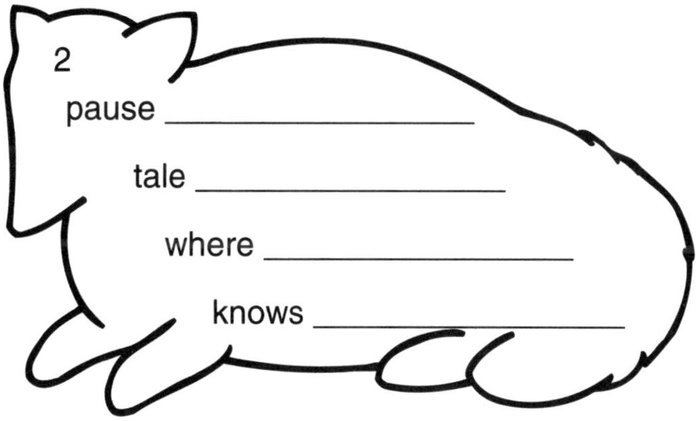

2
- pause _____
- tale _____
- where _____
- knows _____

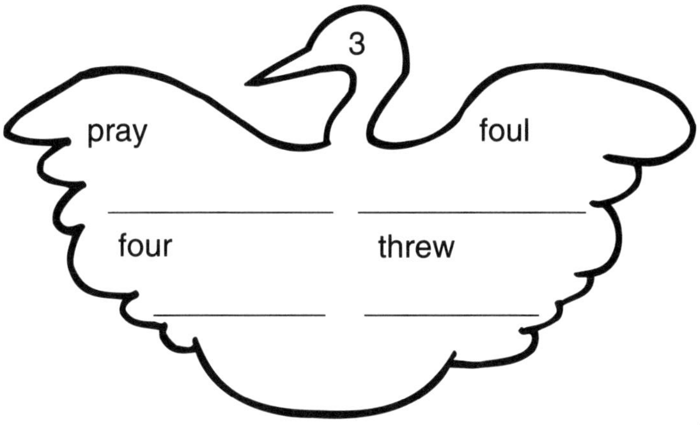

3
- pray _____
- foul _____
- four _____
- threw _____

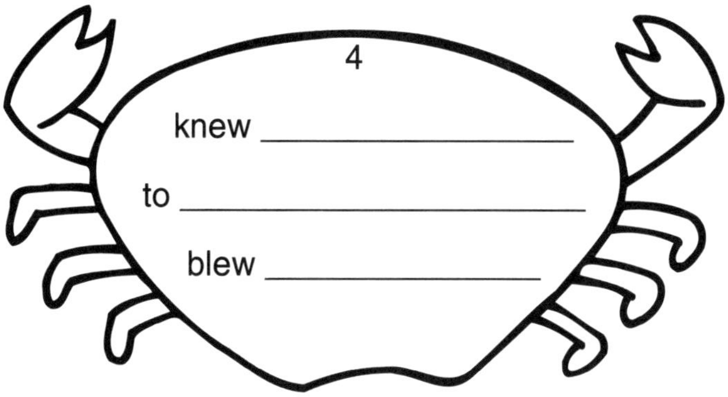

4
- knew _____
- to _____
- blew _____

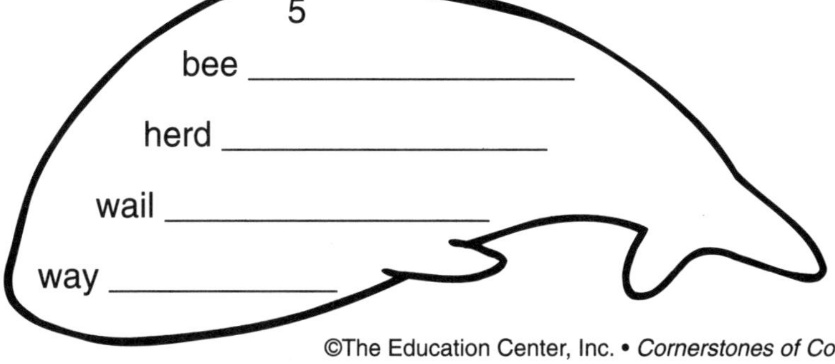

5
- bee _____
- herd _____
- wail _____
- way _____

©The Education Center, Inc. • *Cornerstones of Comprehension* • TEC4103 • Key p. 79

Note to the teacher: Use with activity 4 on page 29.

Animal Alliteration

Alliteration occurs when beginning consonant sounds are repeated in a sentence or a phrase. Here are some examples:

Cautious crabs creep across the coral.   The heron hovers high over the hills.

Directions: For each animal, list verbs, adjectives, and nouns that begin with the same first letter as the animal's name. Use a dictionary to help you. Then write two alliterative sentences in the space provided. The first one has been started for you.

Animal	Nouns	Verbs	Adjectives	Alliterative Sentences
Bear	bashful	befriended	bumblebee	The bashful bear befriended the bumblebee.
Crab				
Fox				
Heron				
Whale				

Note to the teacher: Use with activity 5 on page 29.

The Dog Who Blazed the Westward Trail

Before 1803, land west of the Mississippi River was owned by France. That year, the United States made a deal with France to buy this vast **territory.** President Thomas Jefferson chose Meriwether Lewis to explore the Louisiana Territory. Lewis asked William Clark to help him lead the **expedition.** Lewis also added another special member to the team. His name was Seaman and he was a **Newfoundland** dog. Lewis had paid 20 dollars for his new **companion.**

Perhaps Lewis chose Seaman because of his **breed.** Newfoundlands are very large dogs, but they are usually gentle and friendly. They are good swimmers. Their oily fur keeps water away from their skin. Like others of his breed, Seaman was big and strong. With his thick, wavy fur, he looked a lot like a bear cub. Seaman's shaggy head rose as high as his master's hip. His great tongue looked big enough to lap the frown right off a person's face.

When Lewis bought Seaman, he might have hoped that a dog would be helpful on the trip. He probably did not know just how **valuable** the loyal dog would prove to be. Before long, Seaman showed everyone that he was much more than a pet. He helped provide food for the team of **explorers.** He stood guard over the camp at night. He even risked his own life to protect the men when they faced danger.

There were no stores along the way where the explorers could buy food. However, there was plenty of wildlife on the plains and along the rivers. True to his breed, Seaman went after anything that moved. He chased buffalo. A strong swimmer, he dove from the boat's deck to catch food. He dove into beaver dams and forced the beavers out of their homes. Once, when a beaver was wounded, Seaman swam off to fetch it. The beaver bit into Seaman's back leg to protect itself. Lewis had to work fast to treat the dog's injury. If he didn't stop the flow of blood, Seaman would die.

Luckily for Lewis, the strong Newfoundland survived. Ten days later, Seaman was back at work guarding the camp. One day, as Lewis and Clark slept, a buffalo swam across the river. It **lumbered** out of the water and moved toward the tent. Seaman charged after the beast and forced it to turn just in time. The camp and the men were safe.

Buffalo were not the only danger on the expedition. One dark night, a hungry bear came close to the camp. It **devoured** some buffalo fat that was hanging from a pole. Seaman's barking kept the bear from coming closer to the men. Once again, he kept the camp safe from danger.

Today, a bronze statue in Seaside, Oregon, marks the end of the Lewis and Clark trail. The statue shows Seaman curled up at the feet of Captains Lewis and Clark. His paw rests on a big fish. This brave, shaggy dog traveled down rivers, across plains, and over mountains to the sea. He earned a special place in history as the dog who **blazed** the westward trail with Lewis and Clark. Lewis had paid 20 dollars for the dog, but Seaman proved he was worth his weight in gold.

The Dog Who Blazed the Westward Trail
Activities

1 Predictions

Meriwether Lewis and William Clark were bound to face hardships as they set out to explore the Louisiana Territory. Before students read the selection, partner them and instruct each pair to fold a sheet of lined paper in half lengthwise. Instruct one partner to write a prediction about a challenge the explorers might have faced on one side. On the opposite side, have his partner write a prediction about how Seaman, Lewis's dog, might have helped the explorers face the challenge. Continue until each pair has written three predictions. After students read the selection, have the pair place a check mark beside each confirmed prediction.

2 Multiple-Meaning Words

Use this activity to send students on an expedition for multiple-meaning words. Remind students that some words have more than one meaning. As a class, scan the selection for multiple-meaning words. List the words on the board as they are found. (Multiple-meaning words in the selection include *land, deal, territory, rose, lap, right, trip, guard, turn, safe,* and *curled.*) Invite student volunteers to share at least two meanings for each word. Follow up by having each student complete page 35 as directed.

3 Generalizations

Use this activity to help students bone up on generalizations. In advance, cut a large bowl from colorful paper. Program the bowl with the following statement: "Lewis couldn't have found a better dog than Seaman to take on his journey." Post the bowl where it can be easily viewed by students. Explain to students that the statement is a generalization that expresses the relationship of selection facts and details. Next, have each student cut two bone shapes from white construction paper. Instruct the student to program one bone with a selection detail that supports the generalization and tape it near the bowl. Share students' responses. Direct the student to make a different generalization, based on facts in the selection, on his other bone. Have him add to the back of the bone details that support his generalization. Provide time for students to share their generalizations with the class.

Lewis couldn't have found a better dog than Seaman to take on his journey.

4 Summarizing

Students will give these unique summaries their seal of approval! Write the headings shown below on the chalkboard. For each heading, have the class scan the selection for details. List the details below each heading. Direct each student to write a paragraph using one listed heading and its supporting details. Allow time for students to proofread and edit their work. Then provide each student with a copy of page 36, a 9" x 12" sheet of light-colored construction paper, scissors, and glue. Have students copy their summaries neatly on the lined seal and follow the directions to complete the project. When students are finished, hole-punch the seals, organize them by topic, then slide them onto a metal ring to create a class book.

- Lewis and Clark's Expedition
- Characteristics That Made Seaman a Good Choice for the Expedition
- Ways Seaman Helped Provide Food
- Ways Seaman Protected the Team

5 Similes

The possibilities for writing great similes about Seaman are as plentiful as mosquitoes in summer! Begin by explaining that a simile makes a comparison between two different nouns using the words *like* or *as*. Invite a student to read aloud the selection's second paragraph. Ask another student to identify the sentence containing the simile. *(With his thick, wavy fur, he looked a lot like a bear cub.)* Follow up by having each student complete page 37 as directed. If desired, cut 20 bone shapes from white paper. Program each bone with half of each simile from page 37. Place the set of bones in a center for students to use for practice at a later time.

Name_____   Multiple-meaning words

Are You "Paw-sitive"?

Many of the words we use every day have more than one meaning. Reading the word within a sentence can help you figure out which meaning is being used.

Part 1: Read each sentence. Look at the boldfaced word. Write the letter of the correct meaning in each pawprint.

1. Before 1803, **land** west of the Mississippi River was owned by France.
   R to come to rest in a particular place   N part of the earth's surface

2. That year, the United States made a **deal** with France to buy this vast territory.
   A an agreement   O to distribute playing cards in a game

3. President Thomas Jefferson chose Meriwether Lewis to explore the Louisiana **Territory.**
   P assigned area   T subject of knowledge or interest

4. Lewis probably didn't know just how **valuable** the dog would prove to be.
   I worth a large amount of money   O of great use or service

5. Perhaps Lewis chose Seaman because of his **breed.**
   A to raise plants or animals   E a certain kind of plant or animal

6. Seaman's shaggy head **rose** as high as his master's hip.
   P type of flower   O to move upward

7. His tongue looked big enough to **lap** the frown right off a person's face.
   N to lick   G part of a person's body when seated

8. A strong swimmer, he dove from the boat's **deck** to catch food.
   C part of a house   B part of a ship

9. The beaver bit into Seaman's **back** leg to protect itself.
   O the rear part of a body   K backward in time

10. Lewis had to work fast to **treat** the dog's injury.
    N to care for   W to provide with free food

11. The bear devoured some buffalo fat that was hanging from a **pole.**
    B either of two opposites   P long slender object

12. Ten days later, he was back at work guarding the **camp.**
    U to live temporarily outdoors   A group of people living outdoors

13. Once again, he kept the camp **safe** from danger.
    R free from harm   L place to keep valuables

14. The statue shows Seaman curled up at the **feet** of Captains Lewis and Clark.
    T part of the leg   Y unit of measurement equal to 12 inches

Part 2: Who was the French leader who sold the land that Lewis and Clark later explored? Write the colored letters in order on the lines below to find out.

__ __ __ __ L __ __ __ __ __ __ A __ __ __ __ E

Name _____ *Summarizing*

Summary Seal

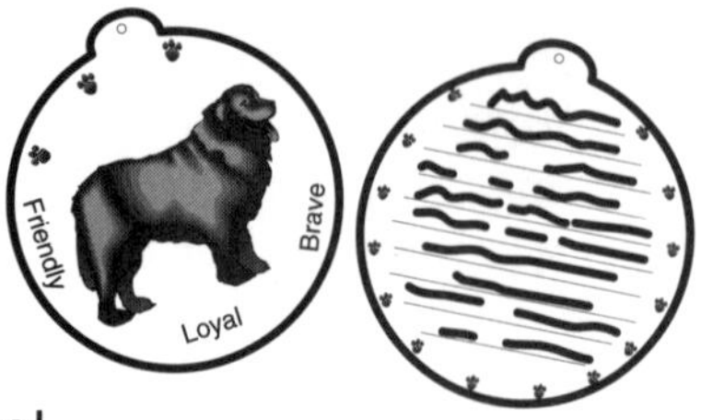

Directions:
1. Copy your summary neatly on the lines provided.
2. Cut out your summary seal along the bold line.
3. Trace the seal on construction paper and cut it out.
4. Glue your summary seal to the back of your construction paper seal.
5. Decorate the front of the construction paper seal to honor Seaman. Be sure to include words and pictures that describe him.

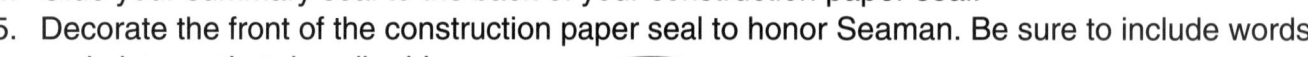

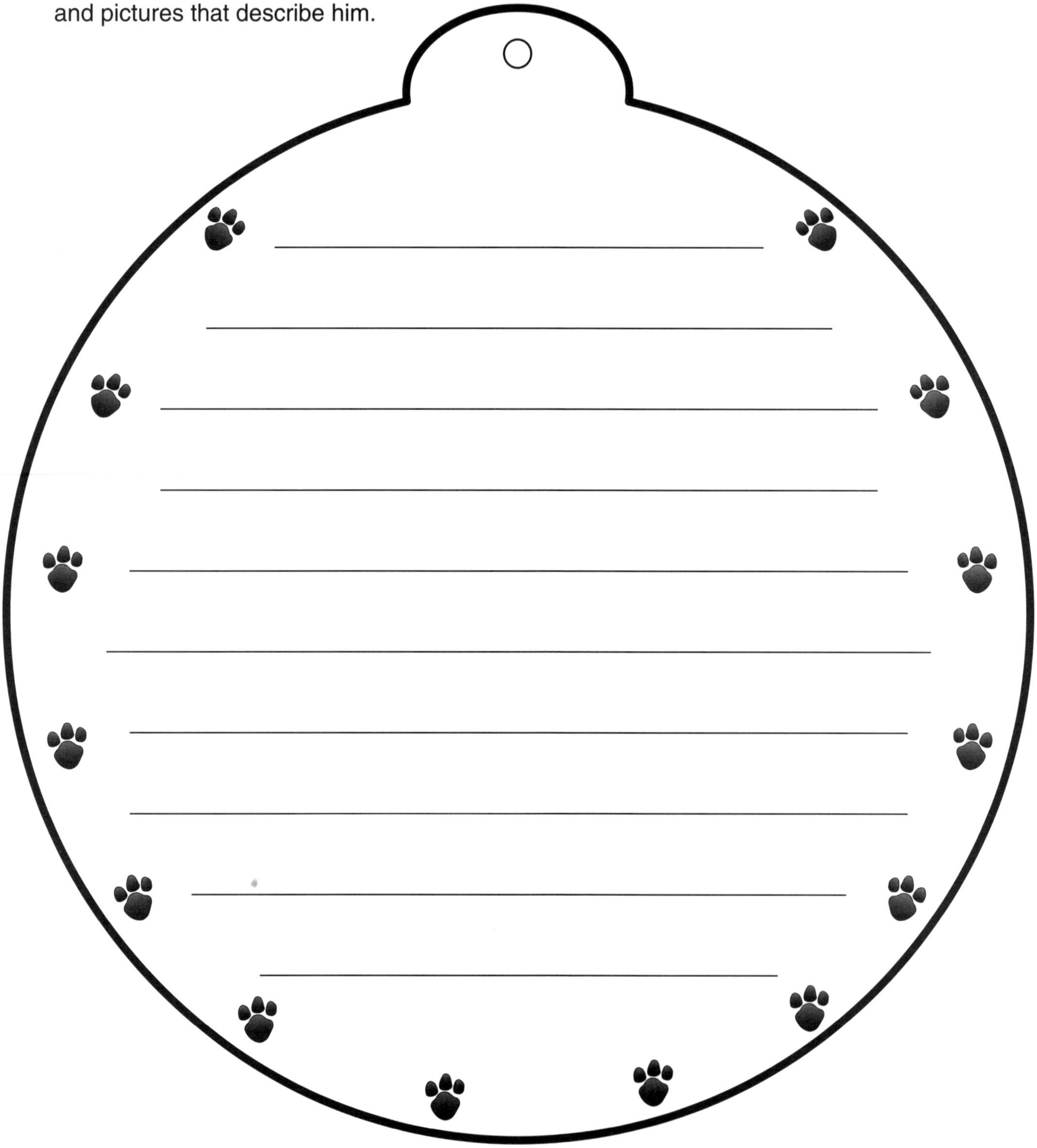

©The Education Center, Inc. • *Cornerstones of Comprehension* • TEC4103

Note to the teacher: Use with activity 4 on page 34.

Name _____

Similes for Seaman

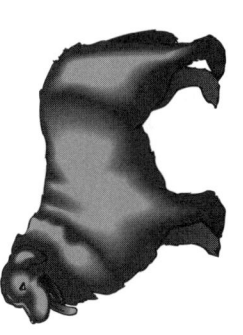

Directions: Read the first part of each simile. Find the phrase that completes each simile on the right. Write the letter in the space provided. (**Remember:** A simile compares two things using the words *like* or *as*.)

Seaman's thick, wavy fur made him look like ____(1)____.

Seaman was as loyal as ____(2)____.

Seaman helped the explorers by hunting the wildlife that was as plentiful as ____(3)____.

His skill as a hunter made Seaman as valuable to the team as ____(4)____.

He snapped up food as fast as ____(5)____.

At the sight of a beaver, Seaman dove into the water like ____(6)____.

When he was bitten by the beaver, Seaman's yelp pierced the air like ____(7)____.

Seaman charged the buffalo like ____(8)____.

Seaman could swim like ____(9)____ and hunt like ____(10)____.

Lewis learned that Seaman was as brave as ____(11)____ and as gentle as ____(12)____.

Cool Connection: On the back of this sheet, write a simile for each of the following words: *Mississippi River, beaver, buffalo, bear.*

A. _____ an otter after a fish

B. _____ a dozen men

C. _____ a lamb

D. _____ a worker bee is to her queen

E. _____ a wolf

F. _____ an angry mother bear protecting her cub

G. _____ a hungry frog snatches a fly

H. _____ a lion

I. _____ a shaggy bear cub

J. _____ mosquitoes in summer

K. _____ an eagle's cry

L. _____ a fish

Note to the teacher: Use with activity 5 on page 34.

Strange, Spooky Spiders

Does seeing spiders send shivers down your spine? Eight legs, sharp fangs, and **poison** glands are enough to give many people that creepy feeling. Add **spinnerets** for weaving webs of sticky **silk**. Then imagine two, four, six, or eight eyes in odd places on its head. This is enough to give some people nasty nightmares!

When we take a closer look, though, we find that spiders are more fascinating than fearsome. Scientists have found more than 30,000 different kinds of spiders. They come in many shapes, sizes, and colors. Some are tiny, smaller than the head of a pin. Others are huge, as large as dinner plates. Their legs may be short and stubby or long and **spindly**. Their bodies may be fat or thin, round or flat. They may be brown, black, gray, pink, or other colors. Some, like the crab spider, even have colors to match their surroundings!

Some spiders look stranger than others. Take the bird-dropping spider, for example. It protects itself by looking like something it's not. This is called **camouflage.** This spider looks like, as its name suggests, bird droppings. Birds eat spiders, but no bird wants to eat one that looks like bird droppings! The spider's strange **costume** helps it in another way too. It can catch an insect for dinner before the insect even knows it's there. Sneaky!

The ogre-faced stick spider looks weird too. It has long, spindly legs and a humped body that looks like a thorn or twig. Two big eyes stick out above its other eyes and make it look like an **ogre** or monster. This spooky spider hides from hungry hunters on tree bark during the day. When the sun sets, it gets ready to hunt. First, it spins a web about the size of a postage stamp. Then it hangs upside down, holding the web with its four front legs. When an unlucky insect passes by, the spider throws the web. The insect is caught like a fish in a net. In a flash, the spider **paralyzes** its victim with poison. Then it wraps the insect in silk like a bug burrito and eats it later. Yum!

Ogre-faced stick spiders aren't the only ones with clever ways of catching food. The raft spider is like an **expert** fisherman. It taps its legs on the water to **lure** small fish and tadpoles to their doom. When a fish swims close to it, the spider dips its head into the water and chomps down. The trap-door spider is very clever too. It builds a door over its tunnel. When an insect passes overhead, the spider runs from its tunnel to catch its meal. Spitting spiders spit sticky silk to catch their prey. The victim is pinned down by the poisonous silk, and this clever spider settles down to its meal.

Most spiders are poisonous but few are able to harm humans. In the United States, harmful spiders include the brown recluse and the black widow. Their bites are painful, but can be treated by doctors. One of the most dangerous spiders is found in South America. The Brazilian wandering spider has been known to hop on board a bunch of bananas. Then a banana boat carries the bananas and spiders to North America. If you find one of these huge, hairy spiders among your bananas, don't make friends. Run!

The truth is that spiders aren't strange or spooky. They have more reason to be afraid of people than we have to be afraid of them. Spiders are interesting and helpful! They build wonderful webs. They eat lots of insects. They are fun to study. Just be careful and watch them from a safe distance. You wouldn't want to make a spider shiver in fear of you!

Strange, Spooky Spiders
Activities

1. Vocabulary

Introduce students to the selection's vocabulary with this clever word web. Ahead of time, stack five 8½" x 11" sheets of paper (Step 1) and draw lines on the top sheet as shown (Step 1). Cut through all five sheets along the drawn lines to create ten web sections. Arrange the pieces in a circle and draw dark lines to resemble a spider web as shown (Step 2).

Divide students into ten groups and assign each group one boldfaced vocabulary word. Provide each group with a web section and have the students write its word in the smallest space. In the middle space, have each group write the definition of its word. In the remaining space, have each group write an original sentence using the word (Step 3). Provide time for each group to introduce its word to the class. Then post the web pieces on a bulletin board titled "Weaving a Web of New Words."

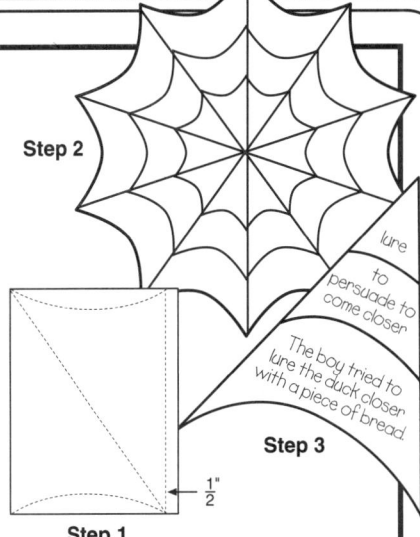

2. Supporting Details

Focus student attention on important details about spiders! Provide each student with a six-inch brown paper circle and eight 1" x 6" strips of brown construction paper. Direct students to scan the selection and write one of the nine spiders mentioned by name on each paper strip. Instruct students to add an important fact about each spider to the back of the labeled paper strip. Have students accordion-fold the strips and attach them with glue or staples around the edge of the circle to form a spider. Provide time for students to decorate their spiders; then display the spiders around the classroom.

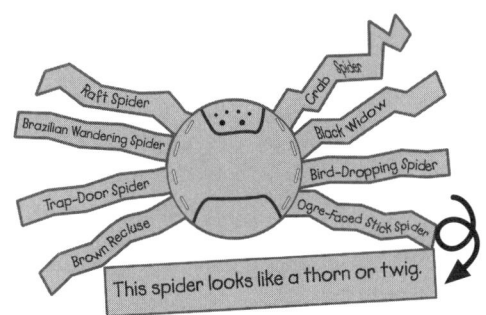

3. Fact and Opinion

The author of "Strange, Spooky Spiders" presents factual information but also includes some opinions. Use this activity to help students develop their ability to distinguish one from the other. Begin by reminding students that facts can be proven or observed and that opinions are related to beliefs or feelings and can't be proven. Invite students to locate and share several facts and opinions from the selection. Then have each student complete the activity on page 40 as directed.

4. Descriptive Language

Writers use a variety of devices to increase understanding and enjoyment for readers. Use this activity to introduce students to two of these devices—simile and alliteration. Begin by reminding students that *alliteration* is the repetition of beginning sounds in two or more words close together. Give the following example: Does seeing spiders send shivers down your spine? Then explain that a *simile* is a figure of speech that makes a comparison using the words *like* or *as.* Give the following example: Some spiders are as large as dinner plates. As students read the selection, have them highlight examples of similes and alliteration. Follow up by having each student complete the activity on page 41 as directed.

5. Point of View

Nothing increases empathy for a spider more than walking around inside its exoskeleton for a day! Begin by explaining that the author of the selection wrote the selection in expository form to give information about a topic. Further explain that the author could have chosen to write a narrative, or story, from a first-person point of view. In that case, the selection would sound like it was told by a spider. Invite each student to pretend to be one of the spiders in the selection. Have each student write a one-day episode in his busy spider life. Share the story starter shown to help students get started. Encourage them to use as much factual information as possible to make their spider stories seem more real.

It's a beautiful day for fishing. Maybe I'll get lucky and catch a tadpole. Hey! Look at me! I could be a drummer in a rock-and-roll band!

Name _____   Fact and opinion

Just the Facts

Order in the court! By order of Judge Spider, you must decide which of the following statements from the selection are *facts* and which are *opinions*.

Facts can be proven or observed.

Opinions are related to beliefs or feelings and can't be proven.

Directions: Read each statement below. If the statement is a fact, circle the spider with a red crayon. If the statement is an opinion, circle the spider with a blue crayon. Use the selection if you need help.

 1. The Brazilian wandering spider lives in South America.

 2. Scientists have found more than 30,000 different kinds of spiders.

 3. Spiders are creepy.

 4. Some spiders look stranger than others.

 5. Spiders have sharp fangs.

 6. Bird-dropping spiders are sneaky.

 7. The ogre-faced stick spider looks weird.

 8. Spiders have clever ways of catching food.

 9. The ogre-faced stick spider holds its web with its four front legs.

 10. The raft spider enjoys fishing for its meals.

 11. A trap-door spider runs from its hiding place to catch its prey.

 12. One of the most dangerous spiders is found in South America.

 13. The brown recluse and black widow are poisonous spiders.

 14. Spiders are interesting and fun to study.

 15. Spiders eat lots of insects.

©The Education Center, Inc. • *Cornerstones of Comprehension* • TEC4103 • Key p. 80

Note to the teacher: Use with activity 3 on page 39.

Name_____   *Descriptive language*

Spinning Sensational Spider Sentences

Authors put an interesting spin on their writing by weaving descriptive language into it. Follow the directions below to learn more about similes and alliteration.

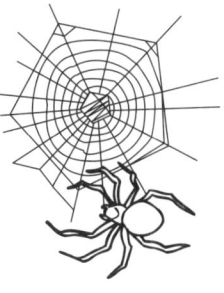

Part 1: Scan the selection to find a sentence in which the beginning sound shown near each spider is repeated two or more times. Copy the sentence on the lines provided and circle the repeated sound. The first one has been done for you.

S

1. Does (s)eeing (s)piders (s)end (s)hivers down your (s)pine?

W

2. _____

H

3. _____

S

4. _____

B

5. _____

W

6. _____

Part 2: Write three original sentences about spiders. Include at least three words with the same beginning sound in each sentence.

1. _____

2. _____

3. _____

Part 3: Locate sentences from the selection that contain similes. Write them on the lines provided. Remember, a simile is a comparison using *like* or *as*. The first one has been done for you.

1. Two big eyes stick out above its other eyes and make it look like an ogre or monster.

2. _____

3. _____

©The Education Center, Inc. • *Cornerstones of Comprehension* • TEC4103 • Key p. 80

Note to the teacher: Use with activity 4 on page 39.

It's Raining! It's Pouring! It's Hopping?

When it rains, people expect to see water fall from the sky. But sometimes they see much stranger things—frogs, fish, and wiggling worms! There have been reports of strange downpours from ancient Egypt to modern England. There seems to be plenty of proof that these tales are true.

Flounders flopping in the streets? Starfish shooting from the clouds? Those and more have fallen in Great Britain during the last few hundred years. The flounders fell on London in 1984. Starfish rained down in North Yorkshire that same year. Tiny frogs the size of beans plopped into puddles in Derby in 1841. A woodworker in Wales was caught out in a strange rain in 1859. While preparing to work with his saw, he felt something falling on his head. He stuck his hand down the neck of his shirt and pulled out a handful of tiny fish. He looked around and saw fish flipping and flopping all over the ground. He filled a bucket with the tiny fish and threw them into a pool to try to save their lives.

Great Britain is not the only place that has **weird** weather. Slimy snails dropped from the sky over Pennsylvania in 1869. Frogs covered Kansas City in 1873. A storm of snakes fell in Memphis in 1876. Sardines fell like silver rain in Australia in 1989. In 1968, **maggots** rained all over a boat race in Mexico. Then, in 1997, toads tumbled from the sky.

Not everything that has fallen from the clouds has been animals. A shower of pennies fell in England for over two minutes in 1956. Did people open their umbrellas? They probably filled their pockets instead! Apples attacked an English couple's house in 1984. They found at least 300 apples in their backyard. They could have baked a lot of pies! Chunks of ice, nails, and bricks have fallen like rain. Even flowers have dropped from the sky!

What causes such weird weather? In 1772, a French group tried to decide why a stone had fallen from the sky. They thought it must have been dug up by **lightning.** After all, everyone knew that there were no stones in the sky. Today we know that stones can fall from the sky. They come from space and are called **meteorites.**

In the 16th century, a scientist claimed that **whirlwinds** probably scooped up things like frogs and fish. Then the wind would dump the little creatures in other areas. Scientists today seem to agree that winds like **tornadoes** and **waterspouts** can cause strange rains. People wonder how the wind can pick up only frogs without picking up mud, fish, and other animals from the same place. No one seems to know the answer.

Perhaps scientists will someday prove what causes strange showers. For now, it may be best to just open an umbrella, watch the sky, and wonder.

It's Raining! It's Pouring! It's Hopping?

Activities

1 Generalizations

Before reading the selection, explain that a *generalization* is a conclusion based on known facts or details. Further explain that a generalization is *valid* if it is supported by facts or evidence and *invalid* if it is not. Tell students that the words *sometimes, most, many, usually,* and *some* are clue words for valid generalizations. Clue words for invalid generalizations include *all, always,* and *never.* As a class, brainstorm things that fall from the sky during storms, such as rain, snow, and hail. Next, guide students to generalize that all things that fall during storms are made of water. As they read the selection, have students think about whether their generalization is valid or invalid. Follow up by having each student complete page 44 as directed.

2 Imagery

"Flounders flopping in the streets? Starfish shooting from the clouds?" The selection is flooded with *imagery,* or descriptions that create word pictures in the reader's mind. Have students find examples of imagery in the selection and discuss how the words work together to create vivid images. Follow up by having each student complete page 45 as directed for practice with imagery in writing poetry. If desired, have each student copy her poem on a cloud-shaped cutout decorated with details from her poem. After students share their poems, display their creations on a bulletin board titled "A Downpour of Poetry."

3 Author's Purpose

Help students identify the author's purpose in writing "It's Raining! It's Pouring! It's Hopping?" with this small-group activity. Remind students that authors write to inform, persuade, or entertain the reader. In this selection, the author combines two purposes—to inform and entertain. Divide the class into groups of four or five students. Provide each group with a 9" x 12" sheet of tagboard. Direct each group to draw and label a chart as shown. Then have students find evidence in the selection showing what the author wrote for each purpose. After each group has recorded its examples on the chart, provide time for each group to share its findings with the class.

To entertain	To inform
• includes fun phrases such as "flounders flopping" and "toads tumbled" • tells what people did as strange things fell like rain	• gives dates and places of strange downpours • tells how scientists explain strange downpours

4 Similes

Students will have a sensational time learning about similes with this activity. Explain to the class that a *simile* makes a comparison using the words *like* or *as.* Then have each student close his eyes and imagine that he is in the middle of a strange downpour as you read aloud the first, second, and third paragraphs. Invite several students to use similes to describe what they saw, heard, or felt. For example, "Sardines tumbled out of the sky like sky divers jumping from a plane." Follow up by having each student complete page 46 as directed.

5 Summarizing

Sum up your study of the selection by having students write a segment for a television show. Divide students into small groups. Have each group write a summary of the selection following the outline below. If desired, have each group present its summary on the imaginary show *Best of Beyond Bizarre.*

First paragraph—introduction to strange, stormy weather
Second paragraph—description of Great Britain's weird weather
Third paragraph—description of weird weather around the world
Fourth paragraph—other fallen items; reason for strange downpours

Name _____   Generalizations

Stormy Generalizations

Directions: Read the generalizations and details below. Decide if each generalization is valid (true) or invalid (not true). Write **V** on the sun if it is valid and **I** if it is invalid. Then write on the raindrops under each cloud the detail numbers that support the generalization as valid or show that it is invalid. One has been done for you. *(Hints: Two of the generalizations are invalid. Each detail may support more than one generalization.)*

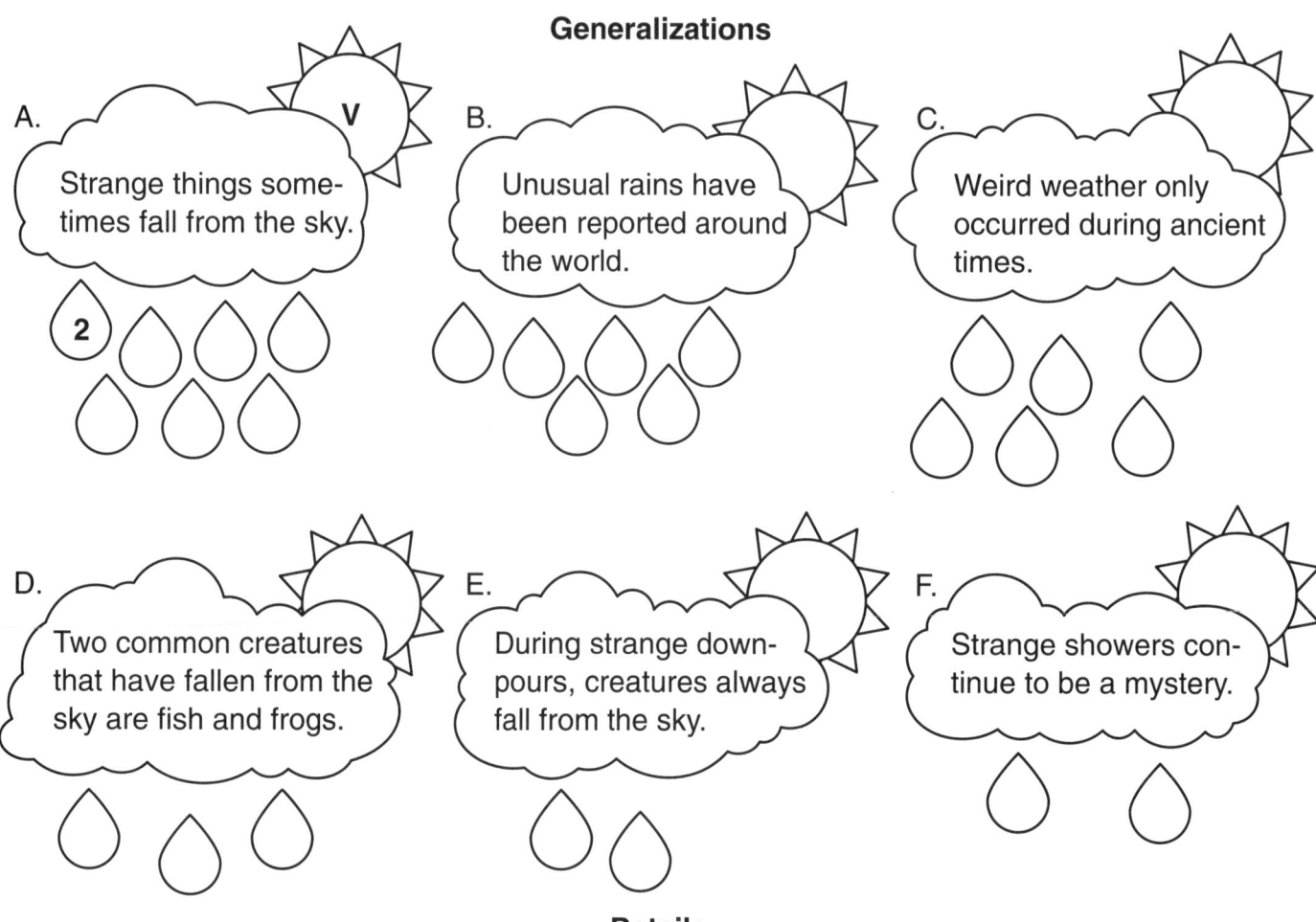

Generalizations

A. Strange things sometimes fall from the sky. (V, 2)
B. Unusual rains have been reported around the world.
C. Weird weather only occurred during ancient times.
D. Two common creatures that have fallen from the sky are fish and frogs.
E. During strange downpours, creatures always fall from the sky.
F. Strange showers continue to be a mystery.

Details

1 Perhaps scientists will someday prove what causes these strange showers.
2 Flounders fell on London in 1984.
3 Apples attacked an English couple's house in 1984.
4 Sardines fell like silver rain in Australia in 1989.
5 In 1968, maggots rained all over a boat race in Mexico.
6 People have seen frogs, fish, and wiggling worms fall from the sky.
7 People wonder how the wind can pick up only frogs without picking up mud, fish, and other animals from the same place.
8 A shower of pennies fell in England for over two minutes in 1956.
9 There have been reports of strange downpours from ancient Egypt to modern England.

Name _____   *Imagery*

Poetic Downpour

Directions: Find six examples of imagery in the selection. Write the phrases on the lines provided on the umbrella. Then use some of the phrases to write an original poem on the lines below. Read the example to help you.

Example:

Raining Fish and Frogs
Toads tumble out of the clouds.
Silver fish fall down like rain.
A shower of pennies draws a crowd.
Such strange events we can't explain!

©The Education Center, Inc. • *Cornerstones of Comprehension* • TEC4103 • Key p. 80

Note to the teacher: Use with activity 2 on page 43.

Sprinkling Similes

Part 1: Read each incomplete sentence below. Look back in the selection and fill in the first blank with the creature or item that fell from the sky. Fill in the second blank with a word from the word bank that completes the simile.

Word Bank
shooting stars   daisies
beans   a blanket
pancakes   jelly
silver streamers

1. _____ flopped like _____ in the streets.

2. _____ as slimy as _____ dropped from the sky in Pennsylvania.

3. _____ fell like _____ in Australia.

4. _____ as tiny as _____ plopped into puddles in Derby.

5. _____ burst from the clouds like _____ in North Yorkshire.

6. _____ covered Kansas City like _____ in 1873.

7. _____ as fresh as _____ attacked an English couple's house.

Part 2: Read each incomplete sentence. Think of a word that completes the simile. Write it on the line.

1. The farmer pulled fish as slippery as _____ from his shirt.

2. Bits of nail as sharp as _____ cut through the sky.

3. Bricks as hard as _____ fell to the ground with loud thumps.

4. Flowers dropped from the sky like _____ from a tree.

Cool Connection: Authors often use similes to create pictures in the reader's mind. Choose one of the similes above. On the back of this page, draw the picture that comes to your mind. Write three sentences to explain how the words created that picture for you.

Watch Out for That Plant!

Certain animals sting, scratch, trap, and eat other animals. Would you expect plants to behave this way? Some do! These plants can be found all over the world. They're not mean. Plants can't run, hide, or hunt so they need other ways to feed and protect themselves.

Some plants do not get all the **minerals** they need from the earth. They are **carnivorous**, feeding on the flesh of animals. Some of these plants grow in **marshes** or **bogs.** Others grow in sandy soil. Some kinds of soil don't provide enough **nutrients** for plants to grow well. Carnivorous plants have adapted to catch insects and use the nutrients found in their bodies.

Are you wondering how plants catch insects? Some use snap traps to catch prey. The Venus's-flytrap belongs to this group. Since it can't chase insects, it **lures** them into its trap. The plant's leaves are covered with sweet nectar. Insects land on the leaves looking for lunch. The instant they touch the three **trigger** hairs on the plant's leaves, the trap snaps closed. It's lunchtime, but not for the insect!

The sundew plant's leaves are covered with sticky hairs that shine like **dew.** If an insect, such as a fly, touches just one of the hairs, it is stuck. As the fly struggles to get free, more hairs slowly curl over it. The sundew has snatched its snack.

Pitcher plants use another kind of trap. Its leaves form a **container** that is shaped like a pitcher. If an insect catches sight of the colorful pitcher, it may land on it. The insect moves toward the sweet smell of nectar. Oops! It slips with a splash into the pool at the bottom of the pitcher. The sides of the pitcher are waxy and slippery so the fly can't climb back out again. Dinner has been delivered to the plant.

Other plants aren't worried as much about eating as they are about being eaten. They protect themselves with a wide variety of weapons. Some plants produce poisons or odors that keep animals away. Others may have spines, spikes, stingers, thorns, or prickles. A person or animal getting too close to one of these plants might get a nasty surprise. Depending on the type of plant, stinging, itching, or burning could be the result of close contact.

Poison ivy is a vine or shrub with shiny green leaves. It grows in parts of America. Its leaves, roots, stems, and fruit contain a poisonous oil that gets on anything that brushes against it. After awhile, the oil can cause itching and redness. Then it can cause oozing **blisters** to appear on the skin. This plant's cousins, poison oak and poison sumac, are shrubs that contain the same harmful poison. It's wise to learn to recognize and avoid all three plants.

The leaves of the stinging nettle have tiny, hollow spikes. If a person or animal touches the plant, the spikes poke **acid** into the skin. This results in a hot, painful rash that can last from an hour to all day. The stinger tree in Australia has an even nastier sting. If touched, the hairs on its leaves shoot poison into the skin like a nurse's needle. Stings from this plant are very painful and can even be deadly.

The skunk cabbage needs to keep animals away so it won't be eaten. It also needs to attract insects to help it make seeds for new plants. Its odor does both jobs. The skunk cabbage smells like—well, a skunk! Some insects are attracted to the awful **stench,** which keeps most animals from eating it. If an animal does nibble on a skunk cabbage, it probably won't like the taste.

Plants can be fun to study. Take a nature walk and look at ways plants feed and protect themselves. Or, adopt a Venus's-flytrap or sundew and watch it eat insects or tiny pieces of meat. Study the amazing ways plants live. But, keep a safe distance from those that sting, scratch, or make you itch!

Watch Out for That Plant!

Activities

1 Vocabulary

Before reading the selection, use this vocabulary activity to sow seeds of understanding. Divide students into small groups. Designate a recorder for each group and provide him with a large index card labeled on the front and back as shown. Assign one boldfaced word from the selection to each group and instruct students to brainstorm their prior knowledge of the word's meaning. Have the recorder write the responses on the card. Next, direct students to use context clues and a dictionary to pinpoint the accurate meaning of the word as it is used in the selection. Have the recorder write the definition on the back of the card. Invite each group to share its work with the class. Follow up by having each student complete the activity on page 49 as directed.

What we know.

What we learned.

2 Supporting Details

After reading the selection, use this activity to organize the details about the plants into an information pyramid. Instruct students to create their pyramids as follows: Write the name of a plant from the selection in section one. In section two, write three words that describe the plant. Write four words that tell how the plant defends itself or traps food in section three. Then in section four, write five words that state another interesting detail about the plant. (The words in each section may make up phrases or sentences.) If desired, have each student write a paragraph about the chosen plant using the details from her pyramid.

Pyramid:
- poison ivy
- shiny green leaves
- poison leaves, roots, stems
- Sumac and oak are cousins.

3 Comparing and Contrasting

Help students recognize likenesses and differences among the plants described in the selection with this activity. Ahead of time, cut out six large construction paper leaf shapes. Label the leaves, each with one of the following: Venus's-flytrap, sundew, pitcher plant, poison ivy, stinging nettle, and skunk cabbage. To begin, tape the leaves onto the chalkboard. Point out that each plant has special characteristics that enable it to capture food, keep predators away, or both. Direct students to reread the selection and decide which of the three best applies to each plant. Record students' responses on the corresponding leaves. Then ask students to find two facts that support their decisions. Record the responses on the leaves. To wrap up the activity, invite a volunteer to the front of the classroom. Give him two of the leaves and ask him to compare the plants, using the information shown. Allow him to choose a volunteer to compare two different plants. Continue until each of the plants has been compared with at least one other. Finally, invite individual students to choose two or three leaves and use the information on them to compare and contrast the plants.

Venus's-flytrap: Venus's-flytrap captures food. It lures insects with sweet nectar. It's leaves close around the insect when the trigger hairs are touched.

4 Cause and Effect

Have students focus on cause-and-effect relationships with this activity. Provide each student with a construction paper leaf. Remind students that *cause* makes something happen and *effect* is the result or outcome. Pair students and direct each twosome to scan the selection and identify an example of cause and effect. Instruct one student in the pair to write the cause on his leaf and the other student to write the effect on her leaf. Then have the pair staple their leaves together with the cause to the left of the effect. Provide time for each pair to share its cause and effect. Then assemble the leaf pairs to form a vine display in your classroom.

Insects touch the trigger hairs on the leaves. The trap snaps closed.

5 Synonyms and Antonyms

Words with synonyms and antonyms pop up like weeds in the selection! Begin by discussing the definitions of *synonym* (a word of similar or like meaning to another) and *antonym* (a word with the opposite meaning of another). Invite students to think of synonyms for words such as *behave* (act) and *provide* (supply). Then ask students to suggest antonyms for words such as *found* (lost) and *more* (less). Instruct students to scan the selection and identify words having synonyms or antonyms. List these on the chalkboard. Then invite a volunteer to "pop up" with a synonym or antonym for each listed word. Follow up by having each student complete the activity on page 50 as directed.

Name _____ Vocabulary

Catch the Meaning!

Trap the meanings of these new words, and don't let them go!

Directions: Read the definition shown under each sundew. Write the matching boldfaced vocabulary word from the selection in the space provided. Use a dictionary if you need help.

1. _____

2. _____

3. _____

Tempts or attracts by offering something as a reward

Raised, liquid-filled wounds caused by irritations or burns

To lead to or be the cause of a sudden action

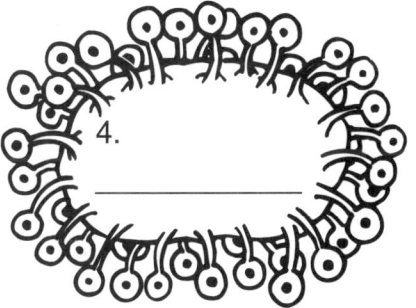
4. _____

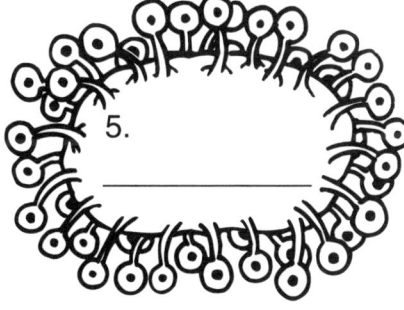
5. _____

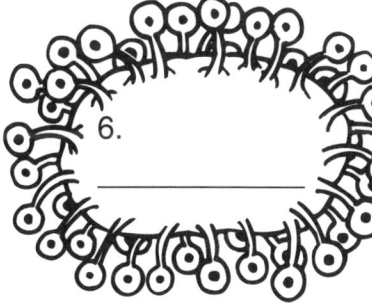
6. _____

Areas of soft, wet land

Feeding on animal flesh

A very bad odor or smell

7. _____

8. _____

9. _____

A chemical substance that has a sour taste

Spongy, soggy areas of ground, often found around large bodies of water

Something that can be used to hold something else, such as a box, bottle, or can

10. _____

11. _____

12. _____

Substances that are needed by a plant or animal, such as vitamins and minerals

Moisture that appears at night on cool surfaces, such as grass and flowers

Natural substances, such as water or sand, that do not come from plants or animals

©The Education Center, Inc. • *Cornerstones of Comprehension* • TEC4103 • Key p. 80

Note to the teacher: Use with activity 1 on page 48.

Name_____ *Synonyms and antonyms*

Plentiful "Plant-onyms"

Directions: One or both words in each of the following pairs are used in the selection. Use context clues to decide if the words are synonyms or antonyms. If they are synonyms, write an *S* on the center leaf. If they are antonyms, write an *A*. The first one has been done for you.

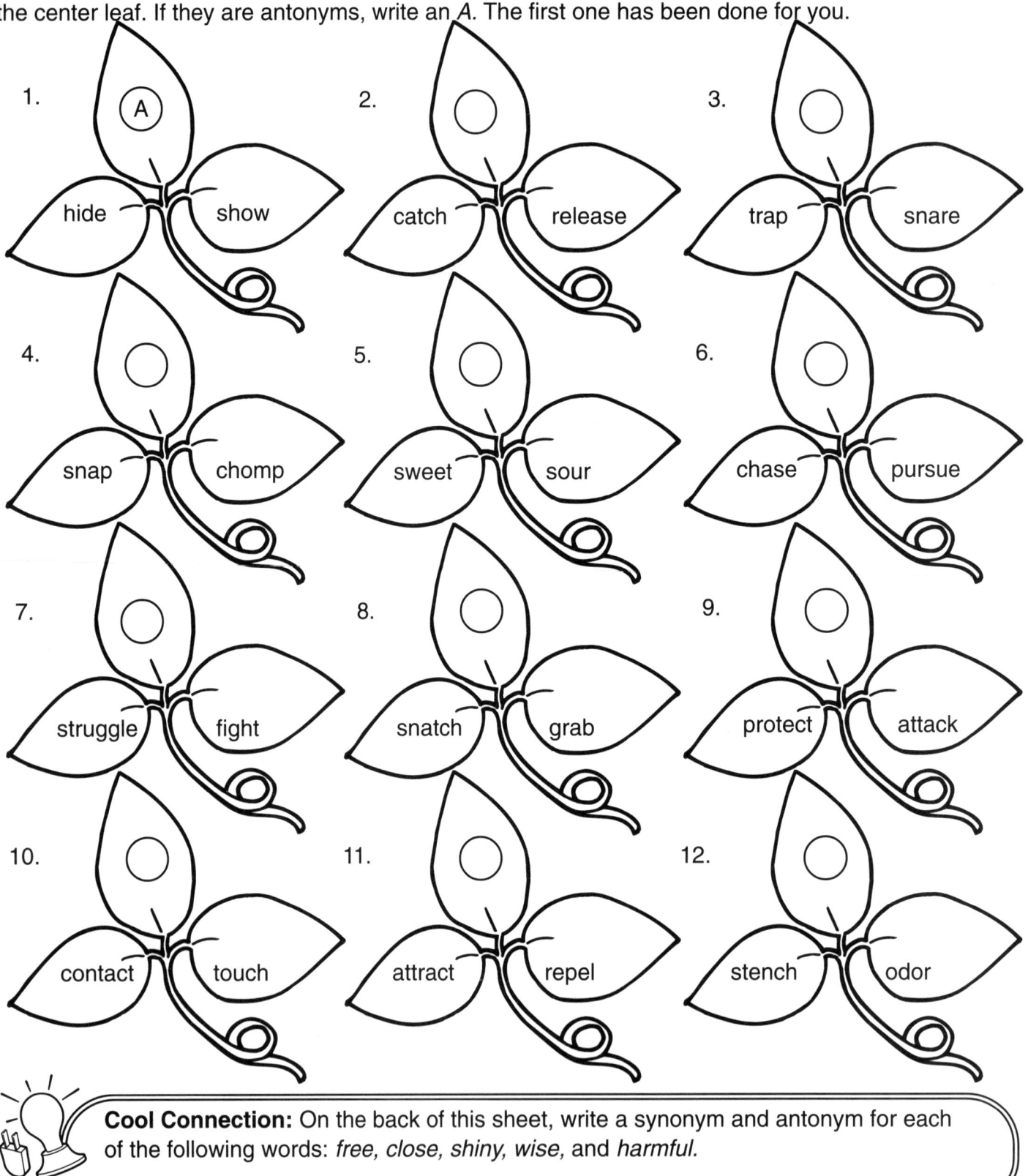

1. (A) hide / show
2. ( ) catch / release
3. ( ) trap / snare
4. ( ) snap / chomp
5. ( ) sweet / sour
6. ( ) chase / pursue
7. ( ) struggle / fight
8. ( ) snatch / grab
9. ( ) protect / attack
10. ( ) contact / touch
11. ( ) attract / repel
12. ( ) stench / odor

Cool Connection: On the back of this sheet, write a synonym and antonym for each of the following words: *free, close, shiny, wise,* and *harmful.*

©The Education Center, Inc. • *Cornerstones of Comprehension* • TEC4103 • Key p. 80

Note to the teacher: Use with activity 5 on page 48.

Attack of the Killer Space Potatoes

It looks like a potato. It's shaped like a potato. It's lumpy, and it has dents that look like the eyes of a potato. Is it a potato? No. It's really a chunk of rock and metal in space called an **asteroid.**

Most asteroids have **irregular** shapes. Since they are often longer than they are wide, many do look a bit like giant potatoes! Some are smaller than raisins. Others are bigger than mountains. These space rocks may have been left over when the **planets** formed.

Asteroids have been called minor planets. Like true planets, they zoom around the sun in paths called **orbits.** They also spin as they speed through space. Most are in an area between the orbits of Mars and Jupiter called the Asteroid Belt. Space rocks in the belt orbit the sun in the same direction as the planets.

Sometimes asteroids change paths. **Gravity,** a force that pulls things together, can cause these changes. The gravitation of large passing planets can slowly pull asteroids into new orbits. If they move into paths used by other space rocks, they may crash. Large asteroids break up when they **collide.** When small asteroids smash into large ones, they often make bowl-shaped holes called **craters.** From a distance, these craters look like the eyes on a potato.

Some asteroids have been pushed or pulled out of the main belt. If they travel too close to a planet or moon, the result could be a crash. Many space rocks have hit Earth's moon. Pictures of the moon show hundreds of craters caused by the impact of space rocks. Sometimes asteroids collide with planets too. They even crash into Earth.

Asteroids that are pulled by Earth's gravity may enter Earth's **atmosphere.** This layer of air works like a shield to protect the planet. Asteroids that are smaller than an office building can't pass through the shield. They burn up in the air. The burning asteroids are called **meteors.** They look like streaks of light as they blaze across the sky. Some people call them shooting stars, but they aren't really stars at all. The thought of fiery rocks falling toward Earth may sound scary. The truth is that most of these beautiful, sparkling visitors are as harmless as the moon.

Some asteroids, though, are deadly. Some scientists think one killer asteroid slammed into the earth 65 million years ago. It may have caused dust and dirt to fill the sky. Sunlight would have been blocked for months. Plants would have begun to die in the darkness. As the plants died, the animals that ate them would have starved. The scientists think that these changes may have led to the death of the dinosaurs.

Could another killer asteroid strike Earth? Scientists say yes. They know that a big space rock has hit our planet an average of once or twice every million years. Teams of **astronomers,** people who study space, keep an eye on asteroids. They have spotted about 1,000 very large space rocks that orbit near our planet. None of these are now on a path toward Earth. Astronomers keep watching, though, because there are still many asteroids to discover.

There is no way to know exactly if or when a giant asteroid might crash into Earth. Scientists have sent spacecraft to study passing space rocks more closely. Scientists hope to use what they learn to find ways to protect our precious planet. One idea might be to use spacecraft to smash asteroids or knock them away from our planet. Perhaps in the future, scientists will be able to turn killer asteroids into mashed space potatoes!

Attack of the Killer Space Potatoes

Activities

1 Vocabulary

Introduce the selection's vocabulary by playing What Goes in the Space? Read the boldfaced words, having students share their prior knowledge of the terms. Then assign one word to each student. Provide her with a sheet of white paper, a dictionary, and crayons or markers. Have her find her assigned word in the selection and copy the sentence containing it, leaving out the word as shown. On the back, instruct the student to write the word's meaning. On the front under the sentence, have her illustrate the word's meaning. Provide time for each student to present her illustration to the class and tell what her word means. Then have her read her sentence and see whether the class can guess the word that should go in the space.

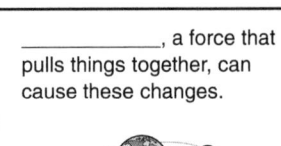
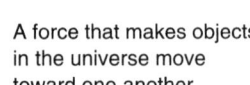

2 Fact and Opinion

Launch students on an exploration of facts and opinions with this activity. Divide the class into small groups. Provide each group with a potato shape cut from 12" x 18" light brown construction paper, six three-inch dark brown paper circles, and glue. Remind students that facts can be proven or observed, while opinions are related to beliefs or feelings and can't be proven. Direct students to scan the selection and write three facts and three opinions, each on a separate circle. Then have them label one side of the paper potato "Facts" and the other side "Opinions." Instruct students to glue each circle on the appropriate side of the potato, arranging the circles to resemble eyes on a potato. Provide time for each group to share its responses.

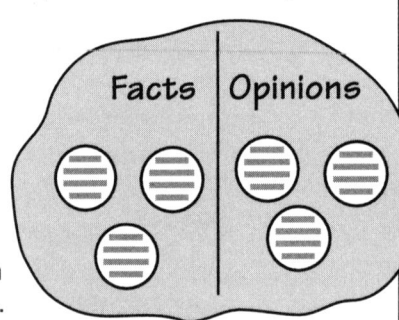

3 Supporting Details

After reading the selection, challenge students to recall details with this Space Potato game. Choose three or four students (space spuds) to sit on chairs (hot seats) at the front of the room. Then have the rest of the class use the selection to make up questions to uproot the students from their chairs. (Students must know the answers to their questions before asking them.) Begin by having a student ask the space spud of his choice a question. If the space spud doesn't know the answer, he loses his chair to the questioner. Expect questioners to dig up questions to stump—and unseat—the space spuds!

4 Multiple-Meaning Words

Send students' vocabularies soaring! Tell students that the word *belt* has several meanings, including "a band of material worn around the waist" and "a closed loop that carries objects." Explain that words or phrases around the word, *context clues,* can help the reader determine the meaning of a word as it is used in a sentence. Have students scan the selection and identify several multiple-meaning words. Invite students to define each word as it is used in the selection and to identify the context clues that helped determine the correct meaning. Follow up by having each student complete the activity on page 53 as directed. (Multiple-meaning words in the selection include *eyes, rock, space, break, spin, crash, blaze,* and *strike*.)

5 Cause and Effect

Have students take a moment to imagine what might happen if a large asteroid crashed into the moon. (A huge crater might be formed. Lots of dust might be thrown into space.) Explain that an *effect* is what happened. (A huge crater formed on the moon.) A *cause* is why it happened. (An asteroid crashed into the moon). Challenge students to scan the selection and identify examples of cause and effect. Discuss their responses. Follow up by having each student complete page 54 as directed.

Name _____   Multiple-meaning words

Multiple-Meaning Meteor Adventure

Study the words shown on the asteroids below. Think about the different ways they can be used. Then read each sentence and match it to the correct definition. Write the letter of the definition on the line provided.

rock
a. to move back and forth
b. stone
c. a form of popular music
1. _____ The astronomer listened to rock as he worked.
2. _____ Asteroids are made of metal and rock.
3. _____ Shock waves from a large asteroid might make buildings rock.

eye
a. organ of sight in people and animals
b. a marking that looks like an eye
c. to look at
4. _____ Scientists eye asteroids through telescopes.
5. _____ A crater on an asteroid looks like the eye of a potato.
6. _____ Jessica saw a meteor out of the corner of her eye.

break
a. to split or crack into pieces
b. to escape by force
c. a brief rest
7. _____ Astronomers need a break after a long night of work.
8. _____ An asteroid will sometimes break up in Earth's atmosphere.
9. _____ Gravity may force an asteroid to break out of its orbit.

make
a. to become
b. to form or shape
c. to add up to
10. _____ If Josh sees one more shooting star, it will make ten.
11. _____ Anna would make a fine astronomer.
12. _____ An asteroid could make a large crater.

spin
a. to create
b. a short trip
c. to turn at a high speed
13. _____ Sophie would like to take a spin in a spacecraft.
14. _____ Asteroids spin as they orbit the sun.
15. _____ I wonder how a spider would spin a web if there were no gravity.

strike
a. to discover
b. to crash into
c. to indicate with a sound
16. _____ Maybe people will strike gold or oil on an asteroid one day!
17. _____ Erin saw a shooting star, just as she heard the clock strike midnight.
18. _____ Scientists think that a giant asteroid might strike Earth.

Cool Connection: Using a dictionary, find a different meaning for each of the words. On the back of this sheet, write a sentence for each word using the meaning you discover.

©The Education Center, Inc. • *Cornerstones of Comprehension* • TEC4103 • Key p. 80

Note to the teacher: Use with activity 4 on page 52.

Name _____   *Cause and effect*

Why Did That Happen?

Directions: Read each cause statement shown on the moons. Find the matching effect statement and write the number in the crater on the matching moon. The first one has been done for you.

1. **d.** When the planets formed, broken remains of large objects were left over.
2. Asteroids spin and revolve around the sun like planets.
3. The gravity of large planets slowly pulls asteroids.
4. One asteroid moves into the path of another.
5. A small asteroid crashes into a large asteroid.
6. Many asteroids traveled too close to the moon.
7. Meteors burn up.
8. Asteroids falling toward Earth burn, making bright streaks in the sky.
9. Earth's moon doesn't have an atmosphere.
10. Many asteroids have crashed into the moon.
11. A killer asteroid may have slammed into Earth 65 million years ago.
12. Some scientists believe that sunlight was blocked by dust for months.

a. Dirt and dust might have filled the sky.
b. Sometimes they are called shooting stars.
c. A crater may form on the large asteroid.
d. Asteroids of all sizes may have formed from these.
e. The two asteroids may crash.
f. Plants would have died. The animals that ate them would have starved.
g. These smaller space rocks can't pass through Earth's atmosphere.
h. Sometimes they are called minor planets.
i. There are lots of craters on its surface.
j. The asteroids crashed into the moon.
k. These asteroids move into new paths or orbits.
l. Asteroids don't burn up before they hit the moon.

Cool Connection: Scientists hope to find a way to protect Earth if a large asteroid comes toward our planet. On the back of this sheet, draw a picture to show a way you think this might be done.

©The Education Center, Inc. • *Cornerstones of Comprehension* • TEC4103 • Key p. 80

Note to the teacher: Use with activity 5 on page 52.

Life on Mars?

People have long wondered if humans are alone in space. Might there be life on other planets? Or is Earth the only planet where living things exist? **Mars** is the fourth planet from the sun. For many years, people have wondered what kinds of things might live there. Books have been written and movies have been made about **Martians,** people who might live on the red planet. Before **space exploration,** no one could prove or disprove the idea that **beings** lived on Mars. Once man began to send spacecraft to Mars, all that changed.

Or did it? The *Viking* spacecraft that flew to Mars in 1976 sent back a picture that stirred up a lot of talk. The photo showed what looked like a huge human face. The face stared straight up into the sky. It had eyes, a nose, and a mouth. Some thought that beings had **sculpted,** or carved, this huge face.

Other shapes near the face did not look natural to some scientists. These shapes looked like **pyramids.** Had beings on Mars built pyramids like those on Earth? No one knew.

What scientists did know was that three conditions must be met for life to exist on a planet. The **temperature** must be right. There must be water. And there must be air. For humans to live on Mars, the red planet must have all three of these things.

Within our **solar system,** only the moon, Earth, and Mars are at the right distance from the sun for life to exist. Though some frozen water has been found on the moon, it has no air. Sometimes it is too hot for life. Sometimes it is too cold. Mars may have some water. It also has milder temperatures on some parts of the planet. But its air is not like the air on Earth. Humans could not breathe there.

The *Viking* spacecraft that landed on Mars in the 1970s did not find any **evidence,** or proof, of life. Some still think that life might have existed on Mars long ago.

If beings ever lived on Mars, did they leave behind a huge face to let others know? The only way to find out was to send another spacecraft to the planet. In 1998, the *Mars Global Surveyor* sent back new photos of the famous face. Though the photos still looked something like a human face, they looked more like an ordinary hill. Scientists believe that the features on the hill were sculpted by running water and windblown sand, not by other life-forms. Even with these new photos, not everyone agrees. Some still believe that the face and pyramids on Mars are **artificial,** not made by nature.

No one knows for sure whether nature or other life-forms made the face on Mars. But another photo sent back to Earth from Mars shows a huge crater that has a circular wall around it. In the middle of the circle is a smile-shaped ridge. Above the smile are two peaks that look like eyes. This face found on Mars is sometimes called the Happy Face Crater. Scientists are certain that this one was made by nature. Maybe nature has a sense of humor too!

Life on Mars? Activities

1 Prior Knowledge

Calling all Martians to complete this red planet K-W-L activity! Before reading the selection, give each student a sheet of red construction paper. Instruct the student to draw and cut out a large circle, then fold the circle into thirds as shown. Have him label the sections as follows: K (know), W (want to know), and L (learned). Explain to each student that he will be reading about Mars and ask him to fill in the K and W sections of his red circle. Direct students to read the selection, filling in the last column with at least five learned details. Provide time for students to share what they learned.

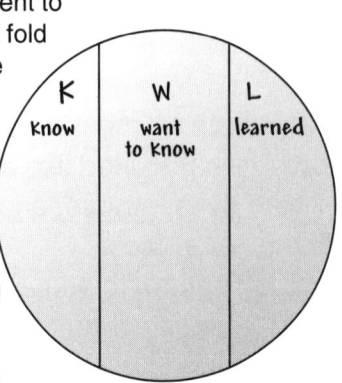

2 Comparing and Contrasting

All budding astronauts in your class will flip over this writing activity. Discuss with students the possibility of life on Mars, pointing out paragraphs four and five from the selection that refer to this. Ask each student to give her opinion on whether life could exist on Mars. Then have each student complete the activity on page 57 to compare and contrast Mars and Earth.

3 Generalizations

Help your students focus on scientific facts and learn about generalizations with this activity. Explain that a *generalization* is a broad statement based on facts. Give the following example: Most scientists agree that the face on Mars is just a group of natural land features. Discuss facts in the selection that support this generalization (see paragraph seven). Then have each student complete the activity on page 58 to learn more about the generalizations in the selection.

4 Fact and Opinion

Launch students on a mission to identify facts and opinions with this game. Give each student four index cards. Instruct the student to write, based on information from the selection, one fact on each of two cards and one opinion on each of the remaining cards. Collect the cards. Divide the class into two teams. Read one statement to the first player of each team. The first player to correctly identify the statement as a fact or opinion gets a point for his team. Continue play until all of the cards have been read.

5 Analogies

Reinforce the vocabulary from the selection with this analogy activity. Explain that an *analogy* shows a likeness between two objects that are otherwise unlike. Give students the following example: *Mars* is to *red planet* as *life-form* is to *being*. Ask students what the relationship is between the sets of words (synonyms). Brainstorm with students a list of other possible analogy relationships, such as those shown. Next, divide students into ten groups. Assign one of the boldfaced vocabulary words or phrases to each group. Have the group write five analogies using its word or phrase. Have groups exchange analogies and figure out the relationship of each.

antonyms	object to place
object to description	cause and effect
part to whole	object to use
object to action	member to group

Name_____   *Comparing and contrasting*

Mars vs. Earth

Mars and Earth are amazing planets. They are similar in many ways. They also have many differences. Follow the directions below to compare these two planets.

Directions:
1. Read the paragraph below about Mars.
2. Think about each fact you have read in the selection and in the paragraph below. If the fact is about Mars *only,* write it in the section of the circle labeled "Mars." If you think it is true about Earth too, write it in the middle section.
3. For each fact listed in the Mars only section, write a contrasting fact about Earth in the Earth section.

Mars

The planet Mars looks reddish from Earth. Its surface includes bright areas, dark areas, and polar caps. The bright areas cover about two-thirds of the planet and are dry, desertlike regions covered with reddish dust. The dark areas cover about one-third of the surface. They are sometimes called *maria,* or seas, even though they don't contain water. The polar caps are located at both the north and south poles. It is thought that they contain large amounts of frozen water. Mars has volcanoes, lava fields, and canyons. Many of its large craters were caused by meteors crashing into the surface. There are three types of clouds on Mars: pink, blue, and white. The pink ones are formed from dust. The blue ones are probably made up of ice crystals. The thick white ones appear to be made up of water vapor.

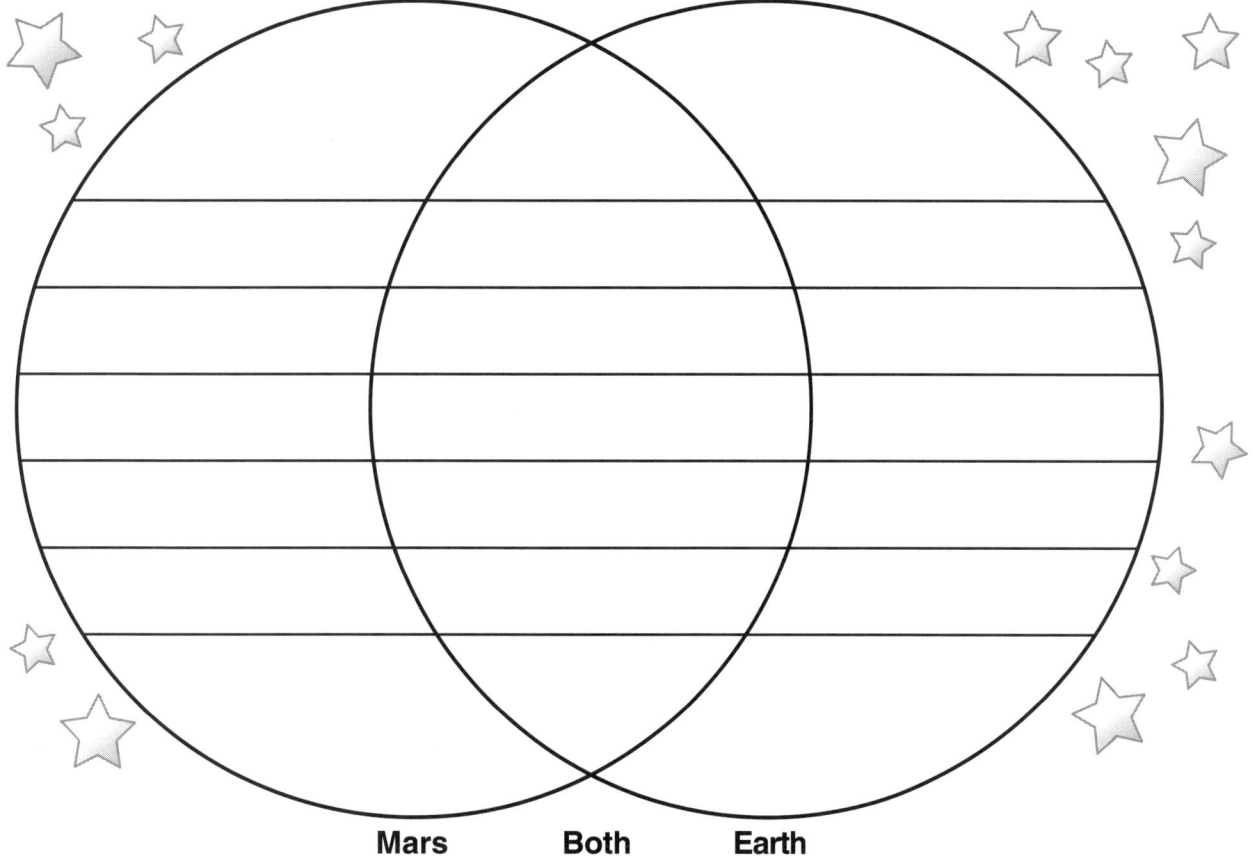

Mars   **Both**   **Earth**

©The Education Center, Inc. • *Cornerstones of Comprehension* • TEC4103 • Key p. 80

Note to the teacher: Use with activity 2 on page 56.

Name _____

Generally Speaking...

Max the "mars-supial" is confused by the generalizations below. He needs the facts to understand what each generalization means. Help Max by following the directions below. Remember, a *generalization* is a broad statement based on facts.

Directions: Read each generalization below. Then find two facts from the selection to support each generalization.

1. It looks like there is a human face on Mars.
   a. _____
   b. _____

2. Certain things are required for life to exist.
   a. _____
   b. _____

3. The moon can't support life.
   a. _____
   b. _____

4. Mars can't support life.
   a. _____
   b. _____

5. Some features on Mars may be artificial and some may be man-made.
   a. _____
   b. _____

Note to the teacher: Use with activity 3 on page 56.

Nessie, Caddy, and Champ

Nessie, Caddy, and Champ sound like names for perky puppies or prize pigs. In fact, they are the names of three mysterious monsters. These lake creatures are said to swim in lakes in Scotland, Canada, and the United States. Many people claim to have seen them, yet no one has been able to prove they exist.

Possibly the most famous is the Loch Ness Monster, whose nickname is Nessie. If a monster wanted to hide in a lake, Scotland's Loch Ness would be the perfect choice. It is deep, long, and narrow. Mountains tower over it, casting shadows over the sometimes **choppy** water. The water is cold and dirty. **Peat,** a form of soft coal, makes the lake so **murky** that it's hard to tell if a monster might be **lurking** in its depths.

Tales of a strange animal in Loch Ness go back many years. One of the earliest sightings dates back to around A.D. 565. Many sightings took place in the 1900s. Two happened in 1933 after a new road was built near the lake. A couple was driving along the eastern shore when a huge gray creature crossed the road in front of them. It had a thick body and a long neck. While driving along the north shore, another couple saw a creature in the lake. It had two humps, together about 20 feet long. In a newspaper story about the sighting, the animal was called a monster. The name stuck. It has been known as the Loch Ness monster ever since.

Most people who claim they have seen Nessie agree that the creature has a small head, a long neck, and a powerful tail. Its large flippers are shaped like diamonds. Some think Nessie is a large **marine** reptile. Others think that a reptile couldn't live in such a cold lake. Then what could Nessie be?

Whatever the creature is, Nessie doesn't seem to be the only one of its kind. For over 300 years, there have been sightings of a monster in Canada's Cadboro Bay. It has been given the nickname Caddy. People say Caddy has a head like a camel, a greenish brown body, and flippers. It is more than 40 feet long. Two scientists have studied sightings and photos of the creature. They reported in 1992 that Caddy might be some type of unknown marine animal.

A third lake monster, Champ, is said to live in Lake Champlain. This large lake is located between New York and Vermont. It is long, narrow, deep, and cold. Local Native Americans told legends about a lake creature dating back hundreds of years. Around 1873, reports of monster sightings started showing up in newspapers. In 1977, a color photo was taken of Champ. It showed something very big that looked like an animal with a small head, long neck, and humped back. Was the picture a **hoax?** Experts said it wasn't a fake. However, the picture doesn't prove that some kind of a lake monster exists.

If Nessie, Caddy, and Champ are real, could they be living dinosaurs? A dinosaur that looked a lot like these lake monsters was the **plesiosaur.** It had a long neck, a small head, and four flippers. The problem is, scientists think plesiosaurs have been **extinct** for more than 60 million years. Could they still exist?

Research teams have used submarines, special cameras, and more to try to solve the mystery of the lake monsters. **Sonar,** a system for finding objects underwater, has been tried also. So far, no real proof has been found. If these marine animals want to stay hidden, we may never be able to prove they exist. Then again, no one can prove that they do not!

Nessie, Caddy, and Champ

Activities

1 Vocabulary

Before reading, "un-loch" the meanings of selection vocabulary. List the selection's boldfaced words on the chalkboard. Pair students and assign one word to each twosome. Direct student pairs to define the words, using a dictionary for help if needed. Then have each pair write three clues to the word's meaning. In turn, invite each pair to read one of its clues aloud. Have remaining students try to identify the matching word from the list. If the answer is correct, the presenting students repeat the word and its meaning. If the answer is incorrect, they give another clue. As each correct answer is given, draw a lake monster shape next to the word on the chalkboard. Follow up by having each student complete the activity on page 61 as directed.

2 Compare and Contrast

Use this activity to help students visualize ways Nessie, Caddy, and Champ are similar and different. Ahead of time, label 12" x 18" sheets of construction paper with three overlapping lakes, creating a Venn diagram. Complete one for each group of three students. Provide each group with a diagram and assign each student in a group one of the three lake monsters. Have each student label one section with her assigned lake monster. Then have students reread the selection and work together to fill in the diagram with details that show similarities and differences among the three creatures.

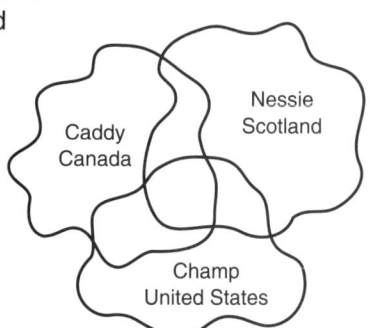

3 Supporting Details

Students will be pleased to plunge into finding details with these pop-up lake monsters. Invite each student to choose one of the monsters described in the selection. Provide her with a 9" x 12" sheet of light blue construction paper, scissors, glue, and scraps of colored paper. Help students create the pop-up cards, following the steps shown below. Have each student write on the cover of her card "Introducing [name of lake monster]!" On the inside, have her write a brief description of her animal using information from the selection. Then have the student create a monster to glue onto the pop-up device. Display the finished creations in the classroom for everyone to enjoy.

Steps for creating the pop-up card:
1. Fold the construction paper in half to 6" x 9".
2. Cut two 1½-inch slits through the fold as shown.
3. Open the paper and push the cut section to the inside.

4 Sequence of Events

Have students take a closer look at the chronology of lake monster sightings. Give each student a Nessie shaped cutout. Divide the class into three sections, having students in each section label their cutouts with one of the monster names (Nessie, Caddy, or Champ). Next, randomly call out a date or time frame from the selection. Have students who are holding cutouts of monsters sighted on or around that date raise them in the air. Ask a student volunteer to scan the selection and describe the sighting. Finally, have students assist you in writing the dates in sequence on the chalkboard. Provide students with scissors, a stapler, and construction paper scraps (at least 1½" x 3½" in size). Follow up by having each student complete the activity on page 62 as directed.

5 Drawing Conclusions

Use the selection to help students draw conclusions about whether these mysterious monsters exist. To begin the activity, have each student decide whether he thinks the creatures are real or just hoaxes. Tell him to scan the selection for evidence that supports his conclusion. Next, have him write an editorial for a fictitious newspaper defending his position. Remind him to use the evidence he found in the selection to support his conclusion. Display the finished editorials on a bulletin board titled "Mysterious Monsters—Real or Hoax?"

Name _____ Vocabulary, context clues

Solving the Mystery of Unknown Words

Help Nessie find and use clues to solve the mystery of the missing words.

Directions: Read each sentence below. Then fill in the blank with the word that best completes the sentence. Underline the clues that helped you decide.

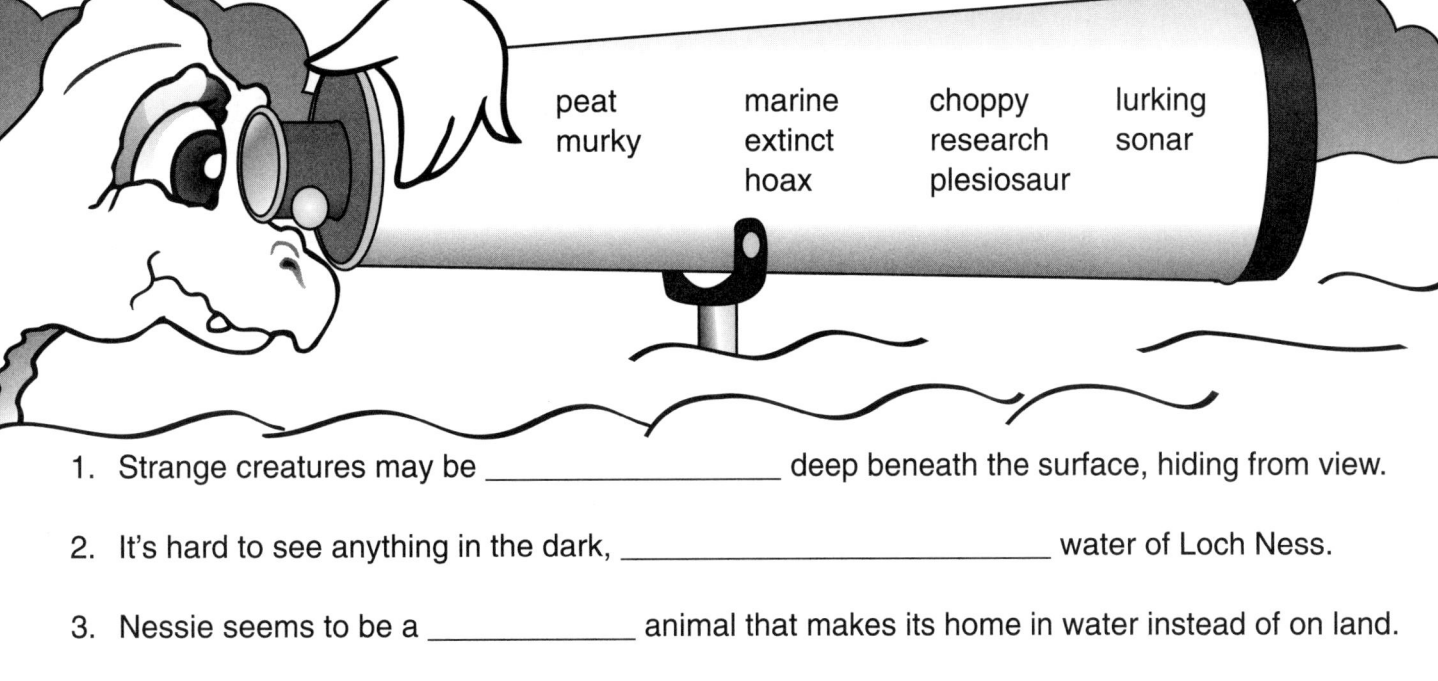

peat   marine   choppy   lurking
murky   extinct   research sonar
        hoax   plesiosaur

1. Strange creatures may be _____ deep beneath the surface, hiding from view.

2. It's hard to see anything in the dark, _____ water of Loch Ness.

3. Nessie seems to be a _____ animal that makes its home in water instead of on land.

4. Is it possible that all dinosaurs are not _____ and that some survive in lakes around the world?

5. A sudden storm on Loch Ness made the water rough and _____ .

6. It has been said that lake monsters look a lot like an extinct dinosaur called a _____ .

7. _____ , a system for finding objects underwater, has been used to try to locate Nessie.

8. Tiny pieces of _____, a form of soft coal, make the water of Loch Ness dark and dirty.

9. _____ teams study as much information as they can gather.

10. One famous _____ was a faked photo of the Loch Ness monster taken on April 1, 1934. April fools!

Cool Connection: Invent a new lake monster and draw it on the back of this sheet. Write a sentence to describe the creature using at least two of the words listed above.

©The Education Center, Inc. • *Cornerstones of Comprehension* • TEC4103 • Key p. 80

Note to the teacher: Use with activity 1 on page 60.

Sequence of Serpent Sightings

Imagine you are doing research on mysterious monster sightings. Follow the directions below to help arrange information about some of the famous sightings for your book on lake monsters and sea serpents.

Part 1: Look at the dates shown on the blank booklet pages below. Use the selection to write about what happened on or near each date. The first one has been started for you.

1933 A couple driving along the north shore of Loch Ness saw a creature that had _____

Around 1873 _____

1977 _____

Around A.D. 565 _____

1992 _____

Over 300 years ago _____

Part 2: Read the following records of additional monster sightings. Then cut out all of the booklet pages and arrange them in order from the earliest to the latest. Create a cover for the booklet and staple the pages together.

1830 Simon's Bay, South Carolina
The captain of a schooner saw a 70-foot monster. Its scaly skin was gray. It had humps and its head was shaped like an alligator's head.

1948 Clearwater, Florida
A large black creature weighing two to three tons was seen waddling near the beach. It left footprints that were 18 inches long, leading in and out of the sea.

1817 Gloucester, Massachusetts
A fisherman reported a 40-foot marine animal in the harbor. It had a dark, triangular head and was making hissing sounds. So many sightings followed that a committee was formed to study the reports.

Note to the teacher: Use with activity 4 on page 60.

Bigfoot Walks

One summer night in 1974, Mike Gordon pulled into the Grays Falls campground. The sun had already set. Mike settled in for the night and went to sleep in his van.

Mike didn't sleep for long. He was jolted awake when the van began to rock. The awful sound of the van being scratched and scraped attacked his ears. Was someone trying to get in? Mike pulled back the van's curtains and peered outside. He was shocked by what he saw.

The **shadowy** figure standing by the van was seven feet tall. In the dim moonlight, Mike could see that the huge creature was covered with hair. Its shoulders were **massive.** Its face was flat, like that of an ape. Mike was scared. What if the beast was trying to get into the van?

Even though he was weak from fear, Mike **scrambled** into the driver's seat. His hand shook as he turned the key. The van's engine ground to life. In the meantime, Mike pounded on the horn. The startled creature bolted into the forest. Mike gunned the engine and headed toward the closest ranger station. He had to tell someone. He had just seen Bigfoot!

Tales of a huge, hairy beast living deep in the forest are nothing new. They go back to before people kept written records. Natives of the United States, Canada, and Asia told stories of a strange, giant creature that walked **upright** like humans. Different groups of people had different names for the beast. Today, the creature is known as *Sasquatch* in Canada and *Yeti* in Asia. In the United States, it is often called *Bigfoot,* a term **coined** by a California man in 1958.

So, just what is Bigfoot? Most people who claim to have seen it agree on many details. To begin, Bigfoot has really big feet! They are from 14 to 22 inches long and five to seven inches wide. Bigfoot walks upright just like an ape or human. At a height of seven to ten feet, Bigfoot would **tower** over most people. It could weigh between 300 and 1,000 pounds. People also say that Bigfoot has long arms, a short neck, and a flat face like an ape's. Its body is covered with brown or reddish fur. Although such a big beast sounds scary, Bigfoot seems to be very shy. If **startled** by a human, it would likely run away (even faster than a person!).

Some think that Bigfoot may be a **descendant** of a giant ape that lived almost two million years ago. Fossil remains of this eleven-foot-tall ape have been found in India, China, and southeast Asia. Did it vanish millions of years ago? Or did it cross the land bridge that once joined Asia and North America and make itself at home in the New World? If so, perhaps the giant ape was the long-lost grandparent of Bigfoot.

Fossils prove that the giant ape lived long ago. So far, there is no real **proof** that Bigfoot exists. No one has ever found Bigfoot's body or bones. Some people have found hair samples and thought they might have come from Bigfoot. However, tests proved that most of the hair came from other animals. Lots of giant footprints have been found. Some were probably prints of bears or other animals. Some footprints have been **exposed** as **hoaxes,** or tricks.

Why do many people still believe Bigfoot is real even though there is no solid proof? With thousands of sightings all over North America, it is hard to prove that Bigfoot is not real. Still, until someone finds proof, this bashful beast will remain one of America's biggest **mysteries!**

Bigfoot Walks

Activities

1 Judgments

Different opinions about Bigfoot's existence are sure to surface after reading this selection. Before reading, label three large index cards as shown. Tape each card in a different corner of the classroom. Ask students whether they believe in the existence of Bigfoot. At your signal, have each child stand in the corner near the sign that indicates his opinion. Have students return to their desks to read the selection. After reading, have students vote again. Ask each child to explain why he did or did not change his vote, citing at least one detail from the selection that changed or confirmed his initial judgment.

2 Supporting Details

Sift through the details of this fascinating selection with a categorizing activity. In advance, cut three large footprints from brown bulletin board paper. Label and display the footprints as shown. After each student reads the selection, have her number the first eight paragraphs on her copy from 1 to 8. Then challenge students to skim the selection for details that fit the footprints' topics. When a student finds a relevant detail, have her identify the number of the paragraph in which it's found, read the detail aloud, and name the appropriate footprint on which to list it. Write the details on the footprints as they are found. Continue until each footprint includes several details.

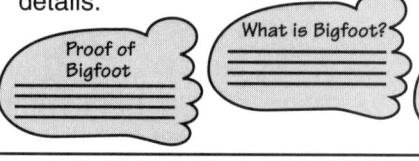

3 Multiple-Meaning Words

Use this activity to take the mystery out of the multiple-meaning words in the selection! List ten of the following words on the board: *set, scrambled, long, saw, figure, face, flat, rock, seat, hand, key, pound, horn, coin, run, fast, tower, cross, land, bridge, hard*. Ask a student to choose one word and write its meaning on the board. Then challenge each student to find the word in the selection, read the sentence that includes it, and decide whether the word's meaning matches the definition on the board. Continue with the remaining words. Follow up by having each student complete the activity on page 65 as directed.

4 Synonyms and Antonyms

Hidden within this selection about elusive Bigfoot are several examples of synonyms and antonyms. After students read the story, discuss the definitions of *synonym*, a word of similar or like meaning, and *antonym*, a word of opposite meaning. Follow up by having each student complete the activity on page 66 as directed.

5 Point of View

Invite students to step into Mike Gordon's shoes with this point-of-view activity. Explain that the author of the selection told about the encounter using the third-person point of view as though he were watching and describing the events. Then explain that if Mike Gordon told the story, he would be using the first-person point of view. Divide the class into groups. Tell students that the man at the ranger station wants Mike to fill out a report about his experience. List the questions shown on the board. Then direct each group to answer the questions in the first person, using appropriate details from the selection. After students have finished, have each team share its answers with the class.

1. Where were you at the time of the incident? What were you doing?
2. Describe what happened, including what you observed and heard.
3. How did you feel during this incident? How do you feel now?

Name _____   Multiple-meaning words

What Big Feet You Have!

Many of the words in "Bigfoot Walks" have more than one meaning. Can you track down the correct definitions for these tricky words? Read each sentence. Draw a big foot in the box beside the correct definition for the boldfaced word.

1. Mike tried to **scramble** into the driver's seat.
   - [ ] to move quickly
   - [ ] to toss or mix

2. The sound of the van's **horn** startled the creature.
   - [ ] antler
   - [ ] device that makes a noise

3. Did you see the creature **bolt** into the forest?
   - [ ] bar or rod used to fasten a door
   - [ ] to dart away

4. The sun had already **set** when Mike pulled into the campground.
   - [ ] to go down
   - [ ] to place with care

5. Did the giant ape really **cross** a land bridge to get to the New World?
   - [ ] to mark out by drawing lines through
   - [ ] to go to the other side of

6. The creature started to **rock** the van.
   - [ ] to cause to shake violently
   - [ ] to surprise or disturb greatly

7. The huge creature would **tower** over most people.
   - [ ] to rise to a great height
   - [ ] tall building or structure

8. It's **hard** to prove that Bigfoot is real.
   - [ ] not easy to break
   - [ ] difficult

9. Who was the first person to **coin** the term *Bigfoot*?
   - [ ] to invent
   - [ ] money

10. Mike was smart to **head** to the ranger station.
    - [ ] to move in a certain direction
    - [ ] chief or principal

Cool Connection: Choose three boldfaced words above. For each word, write a sentence that uses the definition that does <u>not</u> have a big foot. Write your answers on the back of this sheet.

©The Education Center, Inc. • *Cornerstones of Comprehension* • TEC4103 • Key p. 80

Note to the teacher: Use with activity 3 on page 64.

Name _____

Hangin' Around

When Mike Gordon pulled back the curtains hanging on the windows of his van, he was face-to-face with a seven-foot-tall monster—Bigfoot! Are you ready to face this big vocabulary challenge?

Directions: Read the selection word (or form of the word) between each pair of curtains. On the curtains, write two synonyms and two antonyms for the word. Use a thesaurus to help you.

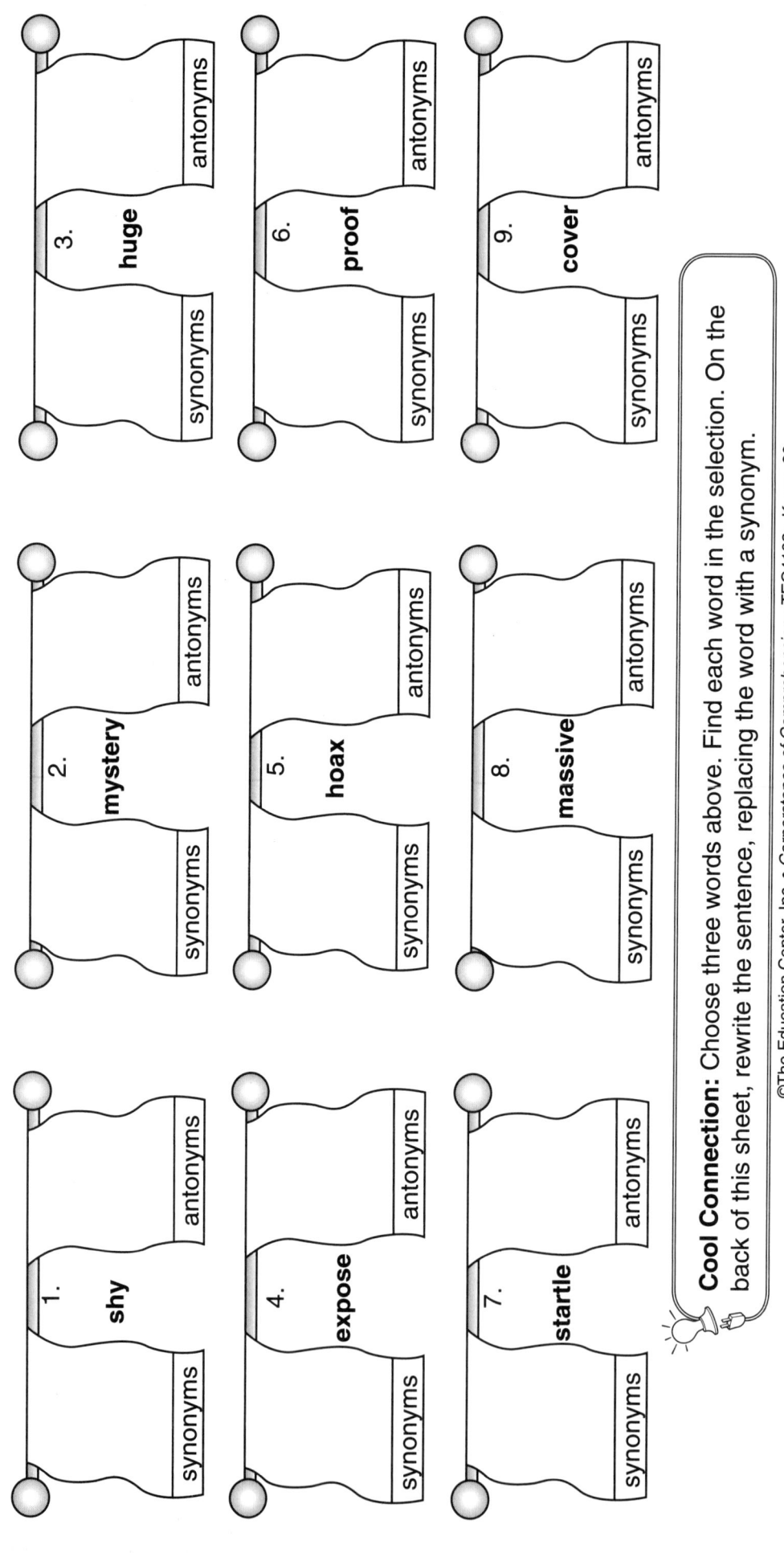

1. shy
2. mystery
3. huge
4. expose
5. hoax
6. proof
7. startle
8. massive
9. cover

Cool Connection: Choose three words above. Find each word in the selection. On the back of this sheet, rewrite the sentence, replacing the word with a synonym.

Note to the teacher: Use with activity 4 on page 64.

©The Education Center, Inc. • *Cornerstones of Comprehension* • TEC4103 • Key p. 80

Flying With Spirit

In May of 1927, Charles Lindbergh arrived at Roosevelt Field. Clouds hung low in the sky. A light rain fell over the **hazy** field. The ground felt soft and muddy. Lindbergh worried a bit about the rain and mud. He had hoped for better weather to begin his flight.

Lindbergh climbed into his tiny plane, the *Spirit of St. Louis.* Sitting inside the **cockpit,** he could reach anything without even stretching his arms all the way out. As the engine roared to life, the plane began to **vibrate.** Its tight fabric skin buzzed. Lindbergh checked the **instruments.** Everything looked fine, but this was no ordinary flight. He was about to attempt to fly nonstop from New York to Paris, France. Other pilots had attempted this **feat,** but none had succeeded. The 3,600-mile flight across the Atlantic Ocean would take about 33 hours. The plane carried 400 gallons of fuel. It felt heavy, like an overloaded truck. Could anything that heavy soar above the clouds?

The engine growled. The plane crept forward, then picked up speed. As Lindbergh pulled back the stick, the wheels left the ground. They touched back down again. After a few bounces, the *Spirit of St. Louis* was **airborne!** Lindbergh was on his way. Would he make it to Paris?

Lindbergh's view of the United States coast faded behind him. Waves danced beneath the plane. Hours later, he was flying above Nova Scotia. Soon after that, he was faced with a pilot's worst nightmare—fog. There were storms too. He picked his way carefully around them. The bad weather had slowed him down, but he was still averaging about 100 miles per hour.

Lindbergh was soon flying over Newfoundland, the last point of land before Europe. Just the cold, dark Atlantic lay before him. Looking down, he saw what he called "white pyramids" of ice. Icebergs! As darkness fell, only a few bright stars shone through the haze.

The dials on the plane's instrument panel glowed like ghostly eyes. Using two **compasses** and the stars, Lindbergh flew on through the night. Hour after lonely hour passed. Suddenly, the plane took Lindbergh into a storm. He decided to try to fly above it. Then, at 10,500 feet, ice formed on the wings. Trying to stay calm, he flew lower where the air wasn't so cold. The ice melted. The plane and its pilot were safe.

Lindbergh's eyelids grew heavy, but he couldn't allow himself to sleep. He knew if he slept that the dark monster below would swallow his plane. He had to stay awake! Trying to keep his mind alert, he guided his little plane high into the sky. Then he dropped it back down toward the **churning** ocean. He held the controls with his right hand, then with his left. He held his eyelids open with his fingers. He didn't eat.

The long night finally turned to dawn. As the sun sent beams of light between the clouds, Lindbergh was filled with hope. Soon, he could see mountains and green fields beyond the foamy coastline. Lindbergh checked his map. He had reached the southern coast of Ireland! Before long, he flew over the steep cliffs of England. At last, he reached France. Night had begun to fall. He could see the twinkling lights of Paris. Lindbergh searched the sky for a **beacon** that would show him where to land. Not finding one, he spotted a large black patch of land that looked like it might be the airport. He was right.

As soon as the plane's wheels touched the ground, a mass of people ran to greet Lindbergh. He had flown nonstop across the Atlantic and into the record books. The newspaper headlines of the day said it best: "American Hero Safe in Paris!"

Flying With Spirit
Activities

1 Vocabulary

Students will flip over this fun vocabulary activity! Provide each student with a 6" x 9" strip of white and a 3" x 6" strip of brown construction paper, a dictionary, scissors, and tape. Have her cut a large white oval shape and gray goggles (like a large capital B). Direct her to place the goggles on the oval and tape them along the top edge. Invite her to add color for skin, hair, and facial features as shown.

Assign one of the selection's boldfaced words to each student and have her write it on the oval beneath the goggles. Then have her write the word's definition on top of the goggles. Group students so that each group has a complete set of the nine vocabulary words. Provide time for each student to read her definition and invite another group member to respond with the word. Have her verify the answer by flipping up the goggles and showing the word.

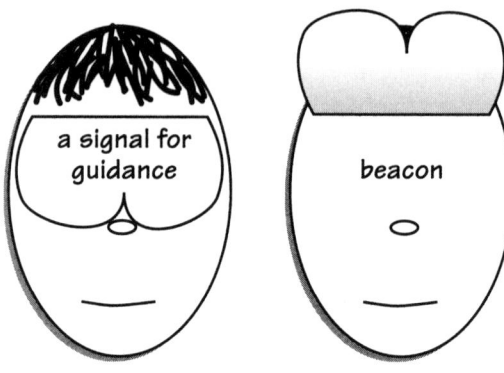

2 Prior Knowledge

Before reading the selection, fuel students' interest in Lindbergh's transatlantic flight by having them map out his journey. In advance, prepare a small construction paper plane cutout. Display a world map. Provide each student with a copy of the selection. Have the class scan the selection and identify the countries over which Lindbergh flew. List the countries on the chalkboard as they are found. Then invite a student to "fly" the plane across the Atlantic on the map, stopping at each country as it is found.

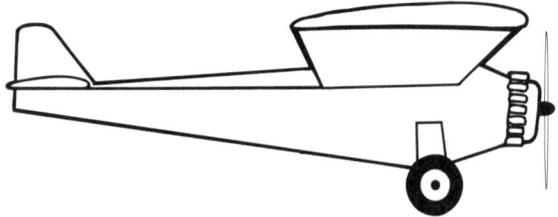

3 Imagery

Descriptive language helps to create images of Lindbergh's flight for the reader. Pair students and provide each twosome with 12 index cards. Direct one partner to write an example of imagery from the selection on each of six cards. Have his partner paraphrase each example without imagery using the six remaining cards. Provide time for students to play a matching game using the cards. To play, have the twosome shuffle the cards and place them facedown on a desk. Tell students to take turns flipping two cards. If the imagery and paraphrase cards match, the student keeps the cards and takes another turn. Otherwise, he flips them back over, and his partner takes a turn. The player who collects more cards wins the game.

| Waves danced beneath the plane. | There were waves under the plane. |

4 Supporting Details

Use this activity to help students take off with relevant and irrelevant details! Remind students that *relevant* details are necessary to tell the story. *Irrelevant* details are not as necessary, but may help to make the story more interesting. Read the following details to students and invite students to tell whether he thinks each is relevant or irrelevant. Follow up by having each student complete the activity on page 69 as directed.

Story details:
A light rain fell over the hazy field. *(irrelevant)*
The 3,600-mile flight across the Atlantic Ocean would take about 33 hours. *(relevant)*

5 Sequence of Events

Deepen students' understanding of sequencing events with this activity. Remind students that *sequence* is the order in which events take place. Begin by asking a student to retell one important event from the selection. Write the response on the chalkboard. Then invite a different student to share an event. Before writing it on the chalkboard, ask the student whether the event occurred before, during, or after the event already posted. Write the response in the appropriate place. Continue in the same manner until four or five events have been listed in sequential order. Follow up by having each student complete the activity on page 70 as directed.

Name _____   *Supporting details*

Daring Details

Sort out the details of Charles Lindbergh's daring trip across the Atlantic!

Directions: Read the pair of statements shown on each plane. Use red to outline the wing that shows the *relevant* detail (important to the story). Use blue to outline the wing that shows the *irrelevant* detail (not as important to the story).

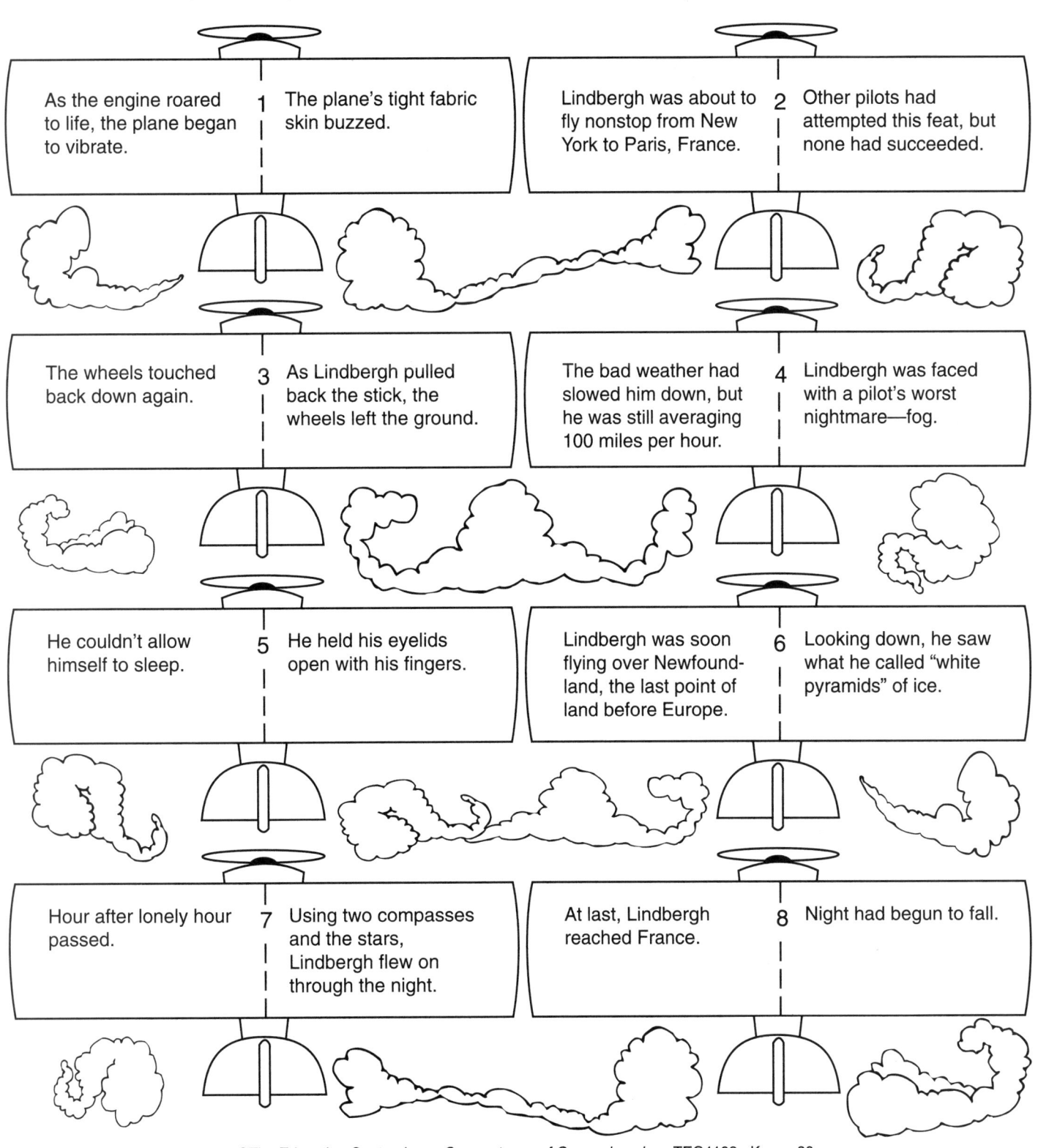

©The Education Center, Inc. • *Cornerstones of Comprehension* • TEC4103 • Key p. 80

Note to the teacher: Use with activity 4 on page 68.

Name _____

Sequence of events

Soaring With Sequence

Directions: Read each of the events shown below. Number them in the order that they occur in the selection. Then write the letter of each event in the correct box on the map showing Lindbergh's route. The first one has been done for you.

a. _13_ The tiny plane touched down in Paris.

b. ____ Lindbergh flew over England.

c. ____ He climbed into the *Spirit of St. Louis*.

d. ____ People ran out to greet the American hero.

e. ____ After a few bounces, the overloaded plane was airborne.

f. ____ Lindbergh could see the southern coast of Ireland.

g. ____ Lindbergh faced dangerous fog and storms.

h. ____ The United States coast faded behind him.

i. ____ Charles Lindbergh arrived at Roosevelt Field in New York.

j. ____ He saw the twinkling lights of Paris.

k. ____ Ice formed on the wings of the plane.

l. ____ Lindbergh flew over Newfoundland, the last point of land before Europe.

m. ____ He searched for a beacon that would tell him where to land.

n. ____ Lindbergh flew over Nova Scotia.

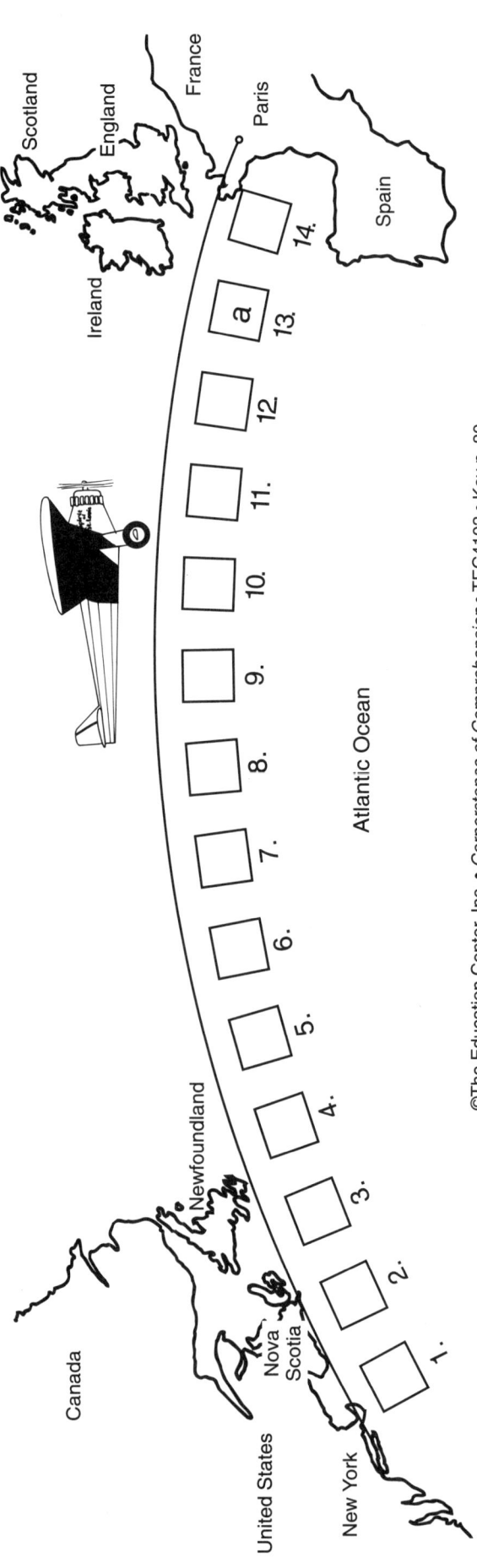

Note to the teacher: Use with activity 5 on page 68.

10...9...8...Danger!

Thousands of people lined the Florida roads and beaches. Millions were watching the event on television. They were waiting for a glimpse of history. Not far away, a giant rocket stood proudly on its launchpad. It towered as high as a skyscraper. On top of the rocket that held the fuel was a command **module.** Three men were strapped inside. Their hearts pounded. Soon, in a burst of flame and smoke, the rocket beneath the astronauts would send them **hurtling** into history. The date was July 16, 1969. The **countdown** to danger had begun.

The three **astronauts** on the *Apollo 11* flight were Neil Armstrong, the commander, and pilots Buzz Aldrin and Michael Collins. Their mission was to land on the moon and then return to the earth. It had never been done before. The men understood the danger. They had just a fifty-fifty chance of coming back to the earth alive.

The countdown drew to the end...10, 9, 8, 7, 6, 5, 4, 3, 2, 1! The giant rocket roared to life. Fire and smoke poured from its base. It lifted heavily from the ground, pushing skyward. The astronauts were pressed into their seats. Moving at 25,000 miles per hour, the rocket shot toward space. It rocked and rolled. It jerked the men left, then right against their straps. Buzz peered out the window and watched Earth fall away beneath them. Would they ever touch it again?

After making 1½ **orbits** around the earth, *Apollo 11* was on its way to the moon. The moon landing was to take place on July 20. That morning, Neil and Buzz climbed into the tiny **lunar** module called the *Eagle*. Neil and Buzz were strapped into a standing position. Belts and cables held them tightly. "You cats take it easy on the lunar surface," Mike joked. Then he pressed his nose against the window and watched the *Eagle* drift away.

The site that had been chosen for the landing was called the Sea of **Tranquility.** Of course, it wasn't really a sea. There isn't any water on the moon. From Earth, the area looked smooth. As the module drew closer, Neil saw that the landing site wasn't smooth at all. It was covered with **craters**—one the size of a football field—and boulders the size of small cars. The module was heading straight into the huge crater. Neil grabbed the controls. Spotting a smooth place, he eased the craft toward the surface. Moon dust spewed up all around as they touched down. "Houston," he said, "...the *Eagle* has landed."

The scientists back at Mission Control could breathe again. "You've got a bunch of guys about to turn blue!" one of them said.

It was time for the greatest adventure of all—stepping onto the moon. The hatch was opened. Neil backed through the tiny opening and down the ladder. As his boot touched the soft, lunar surface he said, "That's one small step for man, one giant leap for mankind." With those words, the crew of *Apollo 11* took its place in history.

By the time Buzz had climbed down the ladder, Neil was acting more like a **tourist** than an astronaut. He had his camera out and snapped a picture as Buzz stepped onto the moon. He kept on taking pictures as he and Buzz worked. They collected rocks and set up experiments. They set up an American flag and even talked to President Richard Nixon.

With the flag flying over the moon's surface and their work done, the astronauts began the long trip home. The heroes of *Apollo 11* returned to Earth on July 24. They had done what people had dreamed of for many years. They had walked on the moon and returned to tell the story.

10...9...8...Danger! Activities

1 Predictions

Point out to students that readers combine details from text and prior knowledge to make predictions. Provide each student with a 4¼" x 11" white paper strip. Have him fold the strip into fourths and label each section as shown. Next, direct the student to draw ½-inch margins along the two middle sections and cut four slits to the drawn lines as shown. Then have him fold the margins to the back and fold back the top corners to make a point.

In the section labeled "What I Know," direct the student to write a fact he already knows about the title. In the section labeled "Predict," have him write what he thinks the selection will be about based on the title alone. Direct the student to read the first paragraph of the selection and revise or confirm his prediction, writing his response in the last section. After reading the selection, have the student confirm or revise his predictions, writing his response on the back of the rocket.

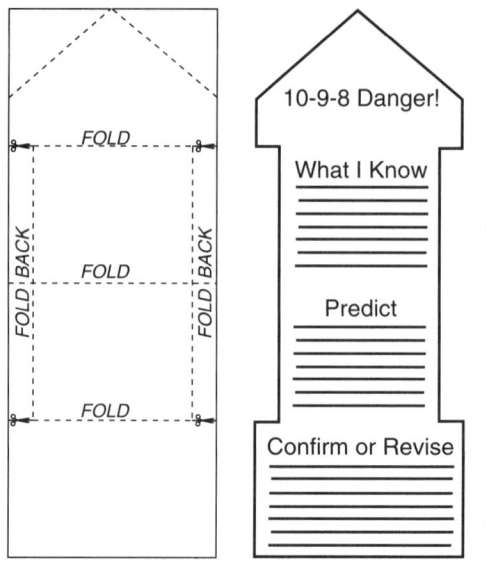

2 Vocabulary

Make it a mission to engage students in meeting and working with vocabulary! Begin by having each student complete the activity on page 73. Advise students to pay close attention to the meaning and spelling of each word. After checking students' answers, divide the class into two teams to play this variation of Hangman as a quick review. Provide each team with a rocket shape that has been cut into five sections. Explain that you will give a definition and a team will spell the associated word aloud. When a team finishes spelling the word correctly, that team tapes one part of its rocket to the chalkboard. The team that completes its rocket first wins the game.

3 Dialogue

Direct quotes from the astronauts and Mission Control help make the selection more interesting and informative. Invite student volunteers to read each of the four quotes aloud and to identify its speaker. Discuss the circumstances that prompted each statement. Provide each student with a 9" x 12" sheet of construction paper and scissors. Direct her to trace the outline of her shoe and to cut out the shape. On the left side of the shape, have the student write the words Armstrong spoke as he stepped onto the moon's surface. On the right side, have her write a statement expressing what she might say if she stepped onto the moon. If desired, display the footprints on a bulletin board prepared to resemble the moon's surface and titled "First Steps on the Moon."

4 Descriptive Language

Towered, hurtling, roared, jerked, peered, spewed, and *snapped* are just a few of the selection's strong verbs that students can use later to energize their own descriptive writing. Divide the class into small groups. Appoint a recorder for each group and provide him with five six-inch yellow circles and a black marker. Direct groups to find five weak or overused verbs in the selection and write them on each circle. Then have group members brainstorm five stronger synonyms for each verb and list them on the back of the circle. Provide time for groups to share their work. Afterward, tape the circles to the ceiling with the strong verbs facing down. Then, by just looking up, students will have a handy reference for strong verbs.

5 Sequence of Events

Recalling the sequence of events helps the reader understand that they are related to each other. Remind students that sequence is the order in which events take place. Ask a student to retell five important events in the selection. Write each response on a separate sentence strip. Then distribute the strips to five students. Have them stand in front of the classroom, holding their event strips so they can be viewed by the class. Invite the remaining students to take turns arranging the events in sequence by directing the standing students to move left or right. Follow up by providing each student with a 9" x 12" sheet of construction paper, scissors, and glue. Have the student complete the activity on page 74 as directed.

Name _____

Vocabulary

A Giant Vocabulary for Mankind

Help the Apollo astronaut collect and identify moon rocks! Write the number of each word on the moon rock that shows its matching definition.

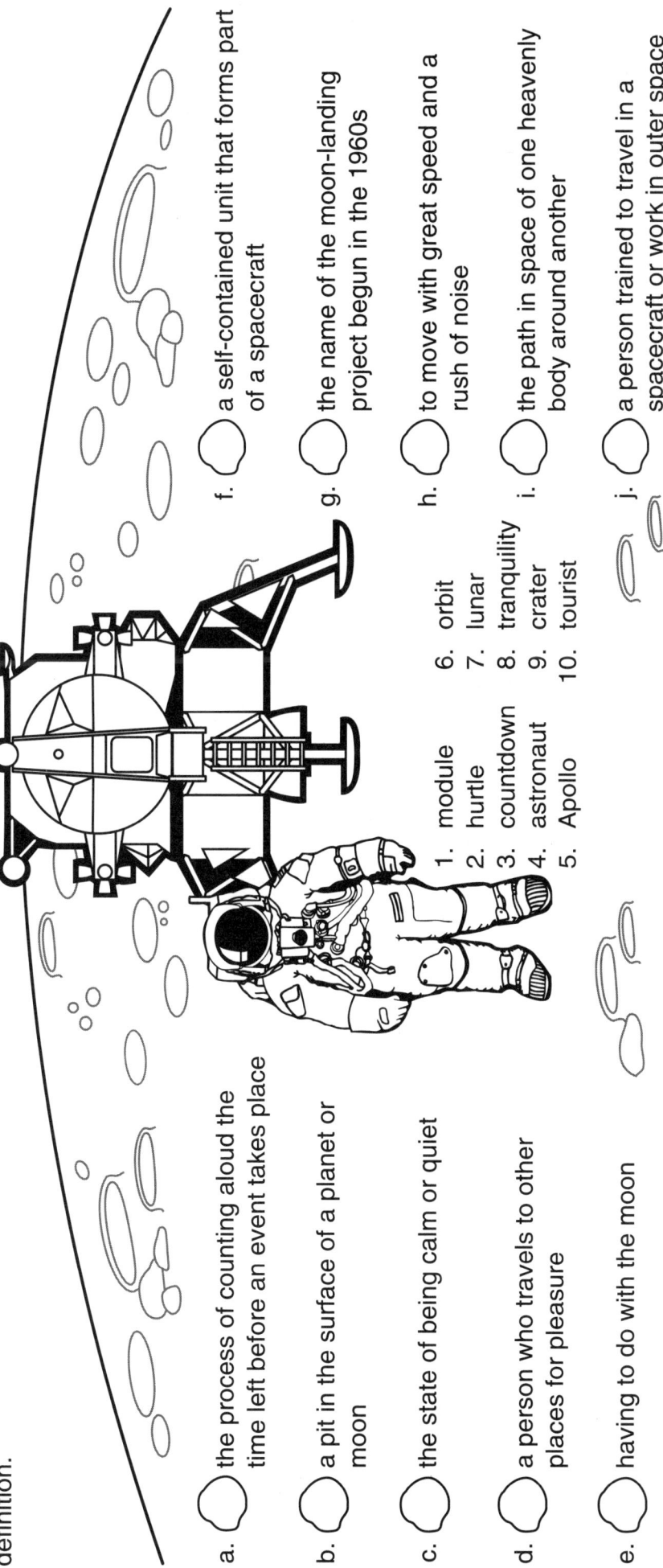

a. ◯ the process of counting aloud the time left before an event takes place

b. ◯ a pit in the surface of a planet or moon

c. ◯ the state of being calm or quiet

d. ◯ a person who travels to other places for pleasure

e. ◯ having to do with the moon

f. ◯ a self-contained unit that forms part of a spacecraft

g. ◯ the name of the moon-landing project begun in the 1960s

h. ◯ to move with great speed and a rush of noise

i. ◯ the path in space of one heavenly body around another

j. ◯ a person trained to travel in a spacecraft or work in outer space

1. module
2. hurtle
3. countdown
4. astronaut
5. Apollo
6. orbit
7. lunar
8. tranquility
9. crater
10. tourist

Cool Connection: If you could be an astronaut, what kind of a mission would you like to go on? Explain your answer on the back of this sheet. Use at least six of the words listed above in your answer.

©The Education Center, Inc. • *Cornerstones of Comprehension* • TEC4103 • Key p. 80

Note to the teacher: Use with activity 2 on page 72.

Name _____   Sequence of events

Countdown of Events

Like any space mission, *Apollo 11*'s journey to the moon began with a countdown for the launch. 10, 9, 8…

Directions: Read the event shown on each moon. Arrange the events in order from the earliest to the most recent and then number them from 1 to 10. Cut out the Saturn V rocket and the ten moons. Glue the rocket to the center of a sheet of construction paper. Then glue each moon next to its matching number on the rocket.

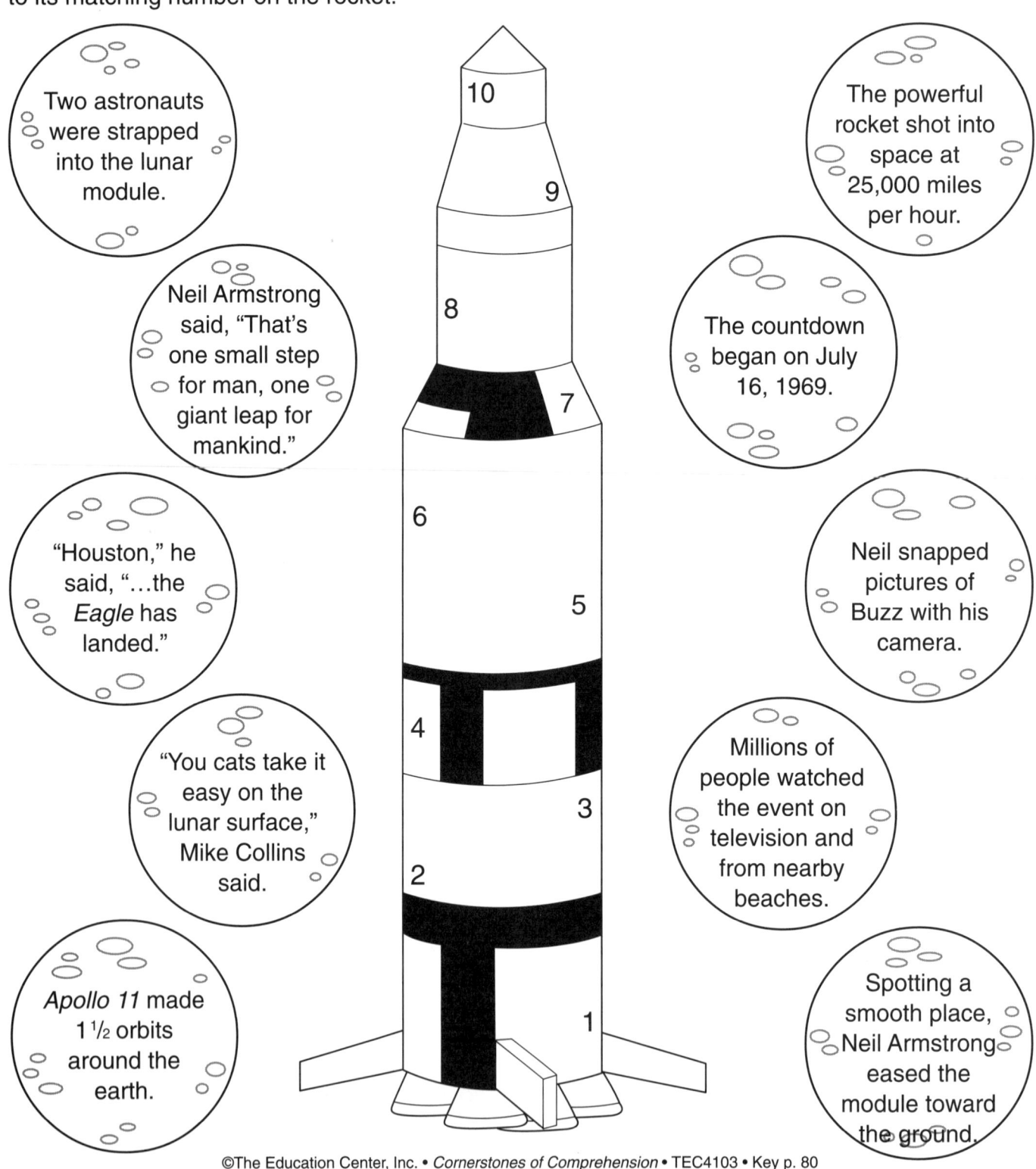

- Two astronauts were strapped into the lunar module.
- Neil Armstrong said, "That's one small step for man, one giant leap for mankind."
- "Houston," he said, "…the *Eagle* has landed."
- "You cats take it easy on the lunar surface," Mike Collins said.
- *Apollo 11* made 1½ orbits around the earth.
- The powerful rocket shot into space at 25,000 miles per hour.
- The countdown began on July 16, 1969.
- Neil snapped pictures of Buzz with his camera.
- Millions of people watched the event on television and from nearby beaches.
- Spotting a smooth place, Neil Armstrong eased the module toward the ground.

©The Education Center, Inc. • *Cornerstones of Comprehension* • TEC4103 • Key p. 80

Note to the teacher: Use with activity 5 on page 72.

Disaster by the Bay

San Francisco was a **bustling** city in 1906. Gold was discovered east of the city in 1848. People headed for San Francisco like flocks of birds. Miners rushed to the area to seek their **fortunes.** It was an exciting place to live. **Cable cars** and **trolleys** prowled like cats up and down the city's steep hills. The city was home to grand hotels and elegant mansions. San Francisco was like a golden **beacon** above the sparkling bay.

Disaster struck as dawn broke over the golden city on Wednesday, April 18, 1906. The earth roared and rumbled like a huge, angry lion. People woke in terror. Still dressed in their pajamas, they scurried like mice from their homes. The ground **buckled** beneath their feet. They fell and couldn't get up again. To stand on that rolling ground was like trying to stand in a canoe on stormy seas.

The earthquake lasted less than two minutes. People gazed around in confusion. Tall buildings became piles of **rubble.** The streets looked like roller coasters with humps and bumps. Railroad and trolley tracks were twisted and useless. Everyone hoped that the worst was over, but danger hissed from broken gas pipes all over the city. Electricity cables that had been snapped by the quake spit sparks. The gas **ignited** and flames spread through the city as if through dry grass.

Horse-drawn fire trucks clattered through the streets. Firemen hooked up hoses, but no water gushed out. The water pipes had been shattered by the earthquake. Men pumped what they could from the **sewers** and from the bay, but they couldn't stop the hungry flames from **devouring** the city.

Jack London, a famous writer, went to San Francisco and wrote about the disaster. He toured the city under the strange red sun. He watched firefighters battle the flames like soldiers bravely facing an enemy. He wrote about their small victories and their great losses. London wrote about the thousands of people trying to get out of the city. Many struggled to heave great trunks filled with household belongings up the hills. Others fled, pulling their treasures in children's wagons or baby buggies. Some people buried their trunks. One man stood in front of a hotel and offered a thousand dollars for a team of horses to take his trunks to safety. There were no horses. Before long, the trunks would be in flames.

For the next few days, the sky itself told the story of the doomed city. The sun was blocked by the smoke that filled the sky. Ashes rained down on the city. In contrast with the thunder of falling buildings, the people seemed strangely silent. The fires raged on. It was Friday before the great war against the fire was won. By that time, the great, golden city had been lost.

The Gold Rush of the 1800s had built San Francisco. Earthquake and fire had turned it to dust and ash. Many people lost their lives in the disaster, and thousands were left homeless. Would the city ever rise again?

There is a myth that tells about a magical bird called the **phoenix.** Every 500 years, the bird is **consumed** by fire and born again from the ashes. San Francisco is like the beautiful phoenix. Within four years, the city had been rebuilt where ashes and rubble once choked the streets. Today, the city shines again above the glittering waters of the bay.

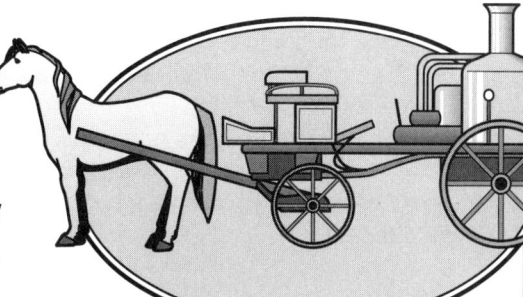

Disaster by the Bay

Activities

1 Vocabulary

To make the reading of the selection run smoothly, begin by using this activity to introduce vocabulary. List the selection's boldfaced vocabulary words on the chalkboard. Read each word aloud with the class. Invite students to share their knowledge of familiar words. (For unknown words, appoint one or more student research assistants to locate the definitions using a dictionary and explain the meanings to the class.) After discussing each word's meaning, ask a student to make up a sentence using the word. Follow up by having each student complete the activity on page 77 as directed.

2 Cause and Effect

Use this activity to help students think critically about the chain of events started by the 1906 earthquake. Remind students that an *effect* is what happened. *(The city of San Francisco was destroyed.)* A *cause* is why it happened. *(An earthquake struck San Francisco.)* Divide the class into eight groups and assign one selection paragraph to each group. Provide each group with two 2" x 11" strips of yellow paper. Instruct group members to reread their assigned paragraph and identify details that describe a cause-and-effect relationship. Direct a member of each group to write the cause on one paper strip and the effect on the other strip. After discussing the responses, connect the strips into a chain and display it in the classroom.

3 Comparing and Contrasting

1906	2003
horse-drawn fire trucks	gas-driven fire trucks
trunks	suitcases
baby buggies	strollers

As they read the selection, did your students notice some of the differences between life today and in 1906? Draw a T-chart on the chalkboard, labeling one side 1906 and the other side with this year's date. Then challenge students to scan the selection and identify details of life in 1906, such as horse-drawn fire trucks, trunks, and baby buggies. On the right side, have students give contrasting details which describe life today, such as gas-powered fire trucks, suitcases, and strollers. Encourage students to add other details from their prior knowledge about ways life has changed over the last hundred years.

4 Similes

"Disaster by the Bay" is like a treasure trove of similes. Use this activity to challenge students to identify similes in the selection and to write some of their own. Remind the class that a simile makes a comparison using the words *like* or *as.* Ask a student to locate the simile in the third sentence of the selection and to read it aloud. Discuss his response. Then challenge students to change the simile by comparing the immigrants to something other than flocks of birds. *(People from all over the world had landed in California like bees on a flower.)* Follow up by having each student complete page 78 as directed.

5 Summarizing

Use this activity to give students practice writing summaries. Point out that if a powerful earthquake occurred today, the news would be reported on television. Divide students into small groups. Have each group write a summary of the disaster in the form of a television news broadcast. Provide time for each group to present its summary on the imaginary show *Yesterday's News Today.*

Name _____ *Vocabulary*

On Track With Vocabulary

Directions: Read the definitions below. Then write the matching boldfaced vocabulary word from the selection in the space provided on the window. Use a dictionary if you need help.

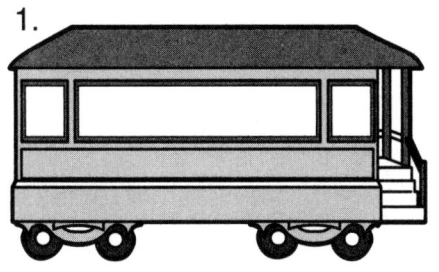
1. Streetcars that run on electricity

2. Completely and totally destroyed

3. Rocks, bricks, or concrete that has crumbled or been knocked loose

4. Busy or moving with great energy

5. A magical bird told about in myth

6. Cars that move by being pulled by cables

7. Eating greedily or destroying

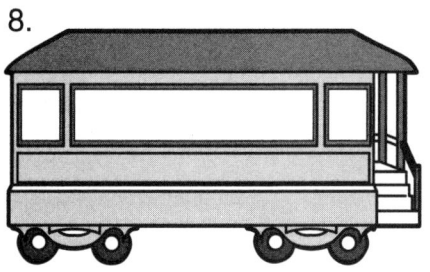
8. Bent or crumpled

9. Something that inspires or guides

10. Underground pipes used to carry waste or rainwater away

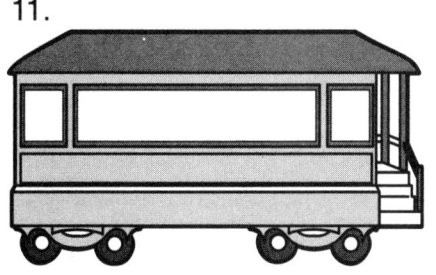
11. Set on fire or caused to burn

12. Wealth, money, or material possessions

©The Education Center, Inc. • *Cornerstones of Comprehension* • TEC4103 • Key p. 80

Note to the teacher: Use with activity 1 on page 76.

Name _____   Similes

A Treasure Trove of Similes

Go on a treasure hunt to search for similes in the selection. Remember, a simile makes a comparison using the words *like* or *as*.

Part 1: Copy a simile from the selection on the lid of each trunk shown below. On the front of the trunk, write a new simile. The first one has been done for you.

1. like flocks of birds / like bees on a flower
2. 
3. 
4. 
5. 
6.

Part 2: Write an original simile about the earthquake on each of the trunks shown below.

7.
8.
9.

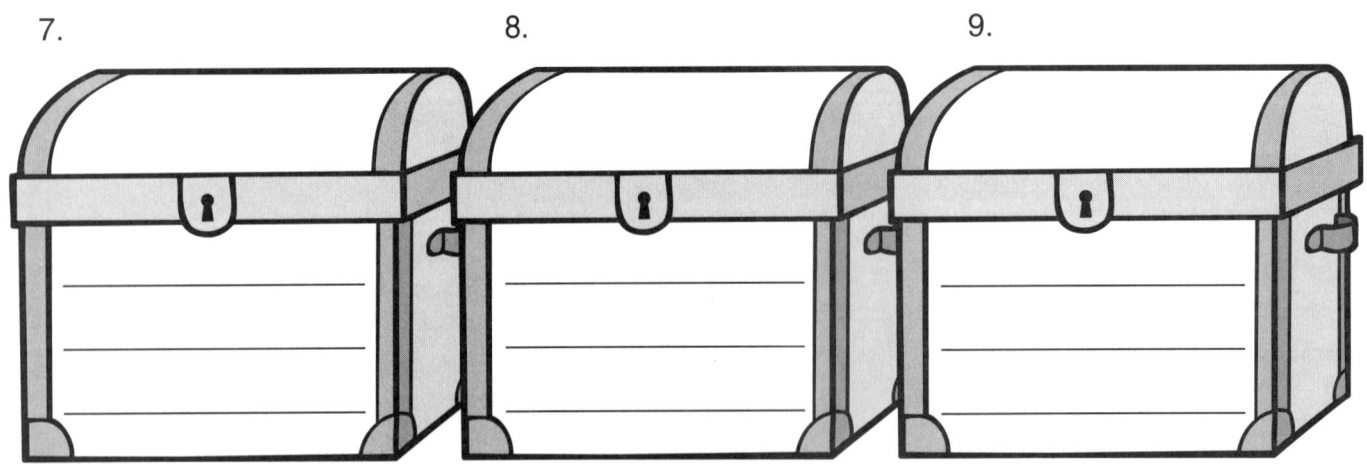

©The Education Center, Inc. • *Cornerstones of Comprehension* • TEC4103

78   **Note to the teacher:** Use with activity 4 on page 76.

Answer Keys

Page 5
A. During the 13 years that Jordan played with the Chicago Bulls, he was named the NBA Most Valuable Player five times.
B. He also became a good student.
   He hoped to go to college when he finished high school.
C. At six feet six inches, Jordan could jump higher than players half a foot taller.
D. Varsity players came to the games to check out his moves.
E. He even made the winning shot at the national championship game.
F. Michael tried out a lot of sports before he settled on basketball.
   He tried football, track, and baseball.
G. They both wanted to be the best.
H. He could wiggle and waggle around in the air.
I. One of his friends said, "If it was a game of Horse and you beat him, you would have to play another game until he won. You didn't go home until he won."
J. He was afraid he'd be a flop.
K. He was upset, but he didn't stop.
   Instead, he worked even harder.
L. They told them not to waste their talent.
M. However, his hard work and will to win launched him right to the top.
N. Jordan once said he sometimes felt like he had little wings on his feet.
O. He pushed his teammates to work as hard as he did.
   He demanded the best of himself and other team members.
P. Jordan once said that somewhere out there is another kid who won't be afraid, a kid who will work hard and build on the example of those who have gone before.
Q. He thought he was too short and skinny to play basketball.
R. In 1996, he was named one of the greatest North American athletes of the 20th century.

Page 6
Responses will vary. Possible responses include the following:
1. Michael and Larry practiced every day.
2. Michael tried other sports before settling on basketball.
3. Michael was surprised when he didn't make the varsity team.
4. He finally made the varsity team.
5. Michael went to the University of North Carolina at Chapel Hill.
6. Michael made the winning shot in a national championship game.
7. Michael left college before his last year to play for the NBA.
8. Michael played for the Chicago Bulls for 13 years.

Page 7

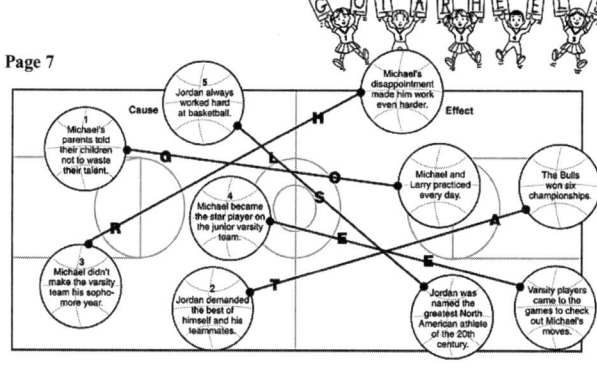

Page 10
Part 1
2. pove(r)ty
3. to(u)rnam(e)nt
4. nati(o)nal
5. at(h)lete
6. cham(p)ionship
7. incre(d)ib(l)e
8. p(r)ofes(s)ional
9. (c)onfe(t)ti
10. bar(e)foot

Part 2
three World Cups

Page 11
Part 1
1. a, b
2. a, c
3. b, c
4. a, c
Part 2
Responses will vary. Possible responses include the following:
1. Pelé was young but was picked because he played so well.
2. He thought it was more important for the team to win than it was for him to play.
3. Pelé's amazing goal scored the winning point in the last game of the tournament.
4. All over Brazil, people were excited to greet the team that had won the World Cup.

Page 14
1. C, publicity
2. D, athlete
3. B, whoop
4. D, silver
5. E, catch
6. B, foe
7. E, tuffet
8. C, popularity
9. A, professional
10. B, earn
11. C, pro
12. A, urge

Page 15
Responses may vary. Possible responses include the following:
Part 1
1. b. Billie Jean played with a dime-store racket.
2. b. Billie Jean had pudgy legs.
3. a. Billie Jean talked to herself on the court.
   b. She even whooped when she won.
Part 2
1. Billie Jean turned out to be a very talented tennis player.
2. Billie Jean wanted to prove that women's tennis was as important and exciting as men's tennis.
3. The match attracted the attention of many people who had never been interested in women's tennis before.

Page 18
Responses will vary. Possible responses include the following:
prophet = green
He could predict the future.
reservation = green
special land set aside for Native Americans
resisting = green
They would not give in.
modest = red
Little Eagle was a show-off.
fearlessly = blue or green
He acted bravely.
fasted = green
He went without food for many days.
warrior = red
peacemaker
charity = blue or green
kindness

Page 19
Responses may vary. Possible responses include the following:
Crazy Horse During Peace
kind—He loved to tell stories to children. He enjoyed teaching the young boys in the village the skills they would need as adults.
modest—Curly was too modest to brag about his bravery when he returned home.
protective—He saw the suffering of his people. Crazy Horse decided to give in and live on the reservation.
Crazy Horse During War
heroic—He led his people into fights against white forces.
brave—He fought fearlessly against an enemy tribe.
stubborn—Crazy Horse refused to move from his native land.
unselfish—He always remembered his vision and, after his first battle, never took anything for himself after a battle.

Page 22
Part 1
Across
3 companion
4 illustrator
7 donate
9 buckle
10 publish
Down
1 nanny
2 embarrass
5 joey
6 character
8 timid
Part 2
Alan Alexander

Page 23
Part 1
1. b
2. c
3. b
4. a
Part 2
Responses will vary. Possible responses include the following:
1. Moon was shy and didn't like getting so much attention.
2. There were some good things about being famous.
3. Moon played with his furry friends so much that they got worn out.
4. A. A. Milne and the publisher thought people might like to see Moon's furry friends.

Page 26
1. H
2. E
3. D
4. G
5. B
6. J
7. I
8. C
9. A
10. F

Page 27
a. Virginia
b. spend
c. young
d. science
e. notebooks
f. letters
g. lawyer
h. pen
i. equal
j. slavery
k. *founded*
l. president

1. *founded*
2. lawyer
3. science
4. president
5. pen
6. Virginia
7. young
8. notebooks
9. spend
10. equal
11. letters
12. slavery

Page 30
Responses may vary. Possible responses include the following:
Glacier or Blue Bear
Habitat—southeast Alaska
Description—heavy, strong body; short legs and large feet; mixture of black and gray hairs
Food—plants, fish, fruit
Interesting Fact—relatives have black, brown, or cinnamon coats

Blue Crab
Habitat—Atlantic coast
Description—ten legs; strong, quick claws; eyes on stalks; hard outer shell
Food—small fish, oysters, clams
Interesting Fact—outgrows and sheds its hard shell

Arctic Fox
Habitat—coastal and inland Arctic areas
Description—bluish gray, bluish black, or white fur; small, round ears; padded feet; bushy tail
Food—fish, rodents, birds
Interesting Fact—fur turns chocolate brown or gray-brown in the summer

Great Blue Heron
Habitat—lakes and marshes
Description—six-foot wingspan; thin, stiltlike legs; long yellow bill; blue-black crown; white crest
Food—fish, lizards, frogs, rodents, insects
Interesting Fact—tries to keep its feathers dry as it wades

Blue Whale
Habitat—ocean
Description—up to 100 feet long, 150 tons or more, strong tail, thin flippers, tube-shaped body
Food—tiny, shrimplike krill
Interesting Fact—loudest cry of any animal on Earth, can be heard thousands of miles away

Page 31
1. fur, bear, see, feet
2. paws, tail, wear, nose
3. prey, for, fowl, through
4. new, two, blue
5. be, heard, whale, weigh
Responses will vary.

Page 35
Part 1
1. N
2. A
3. P
4. O
5. E
6. O
7. N
8. B
9. O
10. N
11. P
12. A
13. R
14. T
Part 2
NAPOLEON BONAPARTE

79

Page 37
1. I
2. D
3. J
4. B
5. G
6. A
7. K
8. F
9. L
10. E
11. H
12. C

Page 40
1. fact (red)
2. fact (red)
3. opinion (blue)
4. opinion (blue)
5. fact (red)
6. opinion (blue)
7. opinion (blue)
8. opinion (blue)
9. fact (red)
10. opinion (blue)
11. fact (red)
12. fact (red)
13. fact (red)
14. opinion (blue)
15. fact (red)

Page 41
Responses will vary. Possible responses include the following:
Part 1
1. Does ⓢeeing ⓢpiders ⓢend ⓢhivers down your ⓢpine?
2. Add spinnerets for ⓦeaving ⓦebs of sticky silk.
3. This spooky spider ⓗides from ⓗungry ⓗunters on tree bark during the day.
4. ⓢpitting ⓢpiders ⓢpit ⓢticky ⓢilk to catch their prey.
5. The ⓑrazilian wandering spider has been known to hop on ⓑoard a ⓑunch of ⓑananas.
6. They build ⓦonderful ⓦebs.
Part 2
1. ⓦeb-ⓦeaving ⓦolf spiders ⓦant ⓦays to catch food.
2. Spider ⓕangs are ⓕearsome and ⓕascinating.
3. The ⓣarantula ⓣickles ⓣom's ⓣoes.
Part 3
1. Two big eyes stick out above its other eyes and make it look like an ogre or monster.
2. The insect is caught like a fish in a net.
3. The raft spider is like an expert fisherman.

Page 44
A. V: 2, 3, 4, 5, 6, 8, 9
B. V: 2, 3, 4, 5, 8, 9
C. V: 2, 4, 5, 8, 9
D. V: 2, 4, 6
E. I: 3, 8
F. V: 1, 7

Page 45
Responses will vary. Possible responses include the following:
flounders flopping
starfish shooting
fish flipping and flopping
a storm of snakes
slimy snails
toads tumbled
sardines fell like silver rain
shower of pennies
apples attacked
whirlwinds scooped up frogs and fish

Page 46
Part 1
1. Flounders, pancakes
2. Snails, jelly
3. Sardines, silver streamers
4. Frogs, beans
5. Starfish, shooting stars
6. Frogs, a blanket
7. Apples, daisies
Part 2
Responses will vary.

Page 49
1. lures
2. blisters
3. trigger
4. marshes
5. carnivorous
6. stench
7. acid
8. bogs
9. container
10. nutrients
11. dew
12. minerals

Page 50
1. A
2. A
3. S
4. S
5. A
6. S
7. S
8. S
9. A
10. S
11. A
12. S

(Page 50 continued)
Cool Connection: Responses will vary. Possible responses include the following:
free: release, capture
close: shut, open
shiny: glossy, dull
wise: smart, foolish
harmful: dangerous, helpful

Page 53
rock
1. c
2. b
3. a
break
7. c
8. a
9. b
spin
13. b
14. c
15. a
eye
4. c
5. b
6. a
make
10. c
11. a
12. b
strike
16. a
17. c
18. b

Page 54
1. d
2. h
3. k
4. e
5. c
6. j
7. g
8. b
9. l
10. i
11. a
12. f

Page 57
Responses will vary. Possible responses include the following:
Mars:
two of the three conditions for life to exist
may have water
air that humans cannot breathe
marias with no water
red
has pink, blue, and white clouds
Both:
mild temperatures
craters
deserts
polar caps
volcanoes, lava, canyons
hills
Earth:
all three of the conditions for life to exist
water
air that humans can breathe
oceans with water
mostly blue in color
white clouds

Page 58
Responses will vary. Possible responses include the following:
1. a. The face stared straight up into the sky.
   b. It had eyes, a nose, and a mouth.
2. a. The temperature must be right to support life.
   b. Water is needed to support life.
3. a. The moon has no air.
   b. Sometimes it is too hot for life.
4. a. Mars may have some water.
   b. Its air is not like the air on Earth.
5. a. The features on the hill may have been made by running water and windblown sand.
   b. Some still believe that the face and pyramids were not made by nature.

Page 61
Underlined responses will vary. Possible responses include the following:
1. lurking, hiding from view
2. murky, hard to see, dark
3. marine, makes its home in water
4. extinct, not, some survive
5. choppy, rough
6. plesiosaur, extinct dinosaur
7. sonar, a system for finding objects underwater
8. peat, form of soft coal
9. research, study
10. hoax, faked photo

Page 62
Part 1
Responses will vary. Possible responses include the following:
1933: A couple driving along the north shore of Loch Ness saw a creature about 20 feet long with two humps. Another couple saw a huge gray creature crossing the road.
Around 1873: Reports of the Lake Champlain monster started showing up in newspapers.
1977: A color photo was taken of Champ. It showed an animal with a small head, long neck, and humped back.
Around A.D. 565: One of the earliest sightings took place.
1992: Two scientists reported that Caddy might be a kind of unknown marine animal.
Over 300 years ago: Since this time, there have been reported sightings of a monster in Cadboro Bay.
Part 2
Order of dates for booklet: around A.D. 565, over 300 years ago, 1817, 1830, around 1873, 1933, 1948, 1977, 1992

Page 65
1. to move quickly
2. device that makes a noise
3. to dart away
4. to go down
5. to go to the other side of
6. to cause to shake violently
7. to rise to a great height
8. difficult
9. to invent
10. to move in a certain direction

Page 66
Responses will vary. Possible responses include the following:
1. synonyms: bashful, modest, timid
   antonyms: bold, brash, forward
2. synonyms: puzzle, riddle, secret
   antonyms: answer, key, solution
3. synonyms: massive, enormous, giant
   antonyms: little, miniature, tiny
4. synonyms: uncover, unveil, reveal
   antonyms: conceal, hide, suppress
5. synonyms: deception, fraud, delusion
   antonyms: candor, honesty, openness
6. synonyms: confirmation, evidence, facts
   antonyms: untruth, misconception
7. synonyms: alarm, amaze, astonish
   antonyms: warn, prepare, signal
8. synonyms: colossal, huge, large
   antonyms: tiny, small
9. synonyms: clothe, conceal, envelop
   antonyms: uncover, bare, reveal

Page 69
Responses may vary. Possible responses include the following:
1. relevant, irrelevant
2. relevant, irrelevant
3. irrelevant, relevant
4. irrelevant, relevant
5. relevant, irrelevant
6. relevant, irrelevant
7. irrelevant, relevant
8. relevant, irrelevant

Page 70
a. 13
b. 10
c. 2
d. 14
e. 3
f. 9
g. 6
h. 4
i. 1
j. 11
k. 8
l. 7
m. 12
n. 5

Page 73
a. 3
b. 9
c. 8
d. 10
e. 7
f. 1
g. 5
h. 2
i. 6
j. 4

Page 74
10. Neil snapped pictures of Buzz with his camera.
9. Neil Armstrong said, "That's one small step for man, one giant leap for mankind."
8. "Houston," he said, "...the *Eagle* has landed."
7. Spotting a smooth place, Neil Armstrong eased the module toward the ground.
6. "You cats take it easy on the lunar surface," Mike Collins said.
5. Two astronauts were strapped into the lunar module.
4. *Apollo 11* made $1\frac{1}{2}$ orbits around the earth.
3. The powerful rocket shot into space at 25,000 miles per hour.
2. The countdown began on July 16, 1969.
1. Millions of people watched the event on television and from nearby beaches.

Page 77
1. trolleys
2. consumed
3. rubble
4. bustling
5. phoenix
6. cable cars
7. devouring
8. buckled
9. beacon
10. sewers
11. ignited
12. fortunes